AMERICAN POETS PROJECT

AMERICAN POETS PROJECT

IS PUBLISHED WITH A GIFT IN MEMORY OF

James Merrill

AND SUPPORT FROM ITS FOUNDING PATRONS

Sidney J. Weinberg, Jr. Foundation

The Berkley Foundation

Richard B. Fisher and Jeanne Donovan Fisher

Carl Sandburg

selected poems

paul berman editor

AMERICAN POETS PROJECT

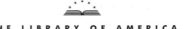

THE LIBRARY OF AMERICA

"Small Homes," "Milk-White Moon, Put the Cows to Sleep," "Slow Program," "Three Slants at New York," "Phizzog," "Two Nocturns," "They Met Young" from *Good Morning, America* copyright © 1928 and renewed © 1956 by Carl Sandburg. Excerpt from *The People, Yes* copyright © 1936 by Harcourt, Inc. and renewed © 1964 by Carl Sandburg. "Brim," "François Villon Forgotten," "The Hammer," "Hammers Pounding," "Dust," "We Must Be Polite," "Two Moon Fantasies" from *The Complete Poems of Carl Sandburg* copyright © 1950 by Carl Sandburg and renewed © 1978 by Margaret Sandburg, Helga Sandburg Crile, and Janet Sandburg. Published by arrangement with Harcourt, Inc.

The paper used in this publication meets the minimum requirements of the American National Standard for Information Sciences—Permanence of Paper for Printed Library Materials, ANSI Z39.48—1984.

Design by Chip Kidd and Mark Melnick.
Frontispiece: Bettmann/CORBIS

Library of Congress Cataloging-in-Publication Data:
Sandburg, Carl, 1878–1967.
    [Poems. Selections]
    Selected poems / Carl Sandburg ; Paul Berman, editor.
        p. cm. — (American poets project ; 23)
    Includes bibliographical references and index.
    ISBN 1-59853-100-X / ISBN 978-1-59853-100-8 (alk. paper)
        I. Berman, Paul. II. Title. III. Series.

PS3537.A618A6 2006
811'.52 — dc22   2006045135

10 9 8 7 6 5 4 3

Carl
Sandburg

CONTENTS

from *Smoke and Steel* (1920)

INTRODUCTION

The line "Hog Butcher for the World" made its debut appearance in 1914 in the opening of Carl Sandburg's poem "Chicago," and a keen-eyed vanguard of readers seems to have recognized right away that here in Sandburg's cheerfully porcine and plebian boast was a phrase for the ages. His admirers, who were many, could get very testy about that line. Even years later, if Sandburg came under attack from some remote and conservative corner of the literary world, the admirers leapt to the assumption that "Hog Butcher for the World" was probably responsible; and if Sandburg needed defense, "Hog Butcher" was the point of departure. I have leafed through the little magazines of the 1910s and '20s looking for the quarrels and discussions that Sandburg aroused, and I have stumbled on an instance of this particular controversy that strikes me as wonderfully revealing—a vivid indication of just how powerful, how thrilling, how transgressive, that single remarkable line used to seem.

This was from 1922 in a literary magazine called *The Double Dealer*, which came out of New Orleans. *The Double*

Dealer was, in its day, mysteriously endowed with the rare and crucial ability to be genuinely up-to-date—the sign of which, in magazines, is invariably a knack for discovering unknown young geniuses from the four corners of the globe. The young William Faulkner accordingly found one of his earliest homes in the pages of the New Orleans *Double Dealer*. Edmund Wilson published a poem in *The Double Dealer* at an age when he was still appending "Jr." to his name. And having opened its pages to Faulkner of Mississippi and to Wilson Jr. of Greenwich Village, *The Double Dealer* decided in 1922 to mount a defense of Carl Sandburg of Chicago—not because Sandburg was young and unknown (he was born in 1878, which made him solidly middle-aged by then) but because that one famous line about hog-butchering in Chicago was still igniting polemics.

The magazine pointed an accusatory finger at the University of Pennsylvania. A well-known literature professor there named Felix Schelling had issued a verdict on Sandburg: "just a man who sets out to find ugly things and to tell about them in an ugly way." And *The Double Dealer*, in its militant up-to-dateness, was aghast. The magazine wondered why a cultivated person, a Shakespeare expert, a scholar respected by poets, would arrive at such a misinformed and ill-considered view. This was a big question. And the magazine published two responses, one in the February 1922 issue and another in May.

February's response stressed the malign role of "snobbishness." The magazine took note of Sandburg's main books (*Chicago Poems*, *Cornhuskers*, *Smoke and Steel*) and figured that Professor Schelling simply could not make his way through the pages. The professor, in the magazine's supposition, "spied the word 'hog-butcher' and was shocked into a conviction which he could not change though he read every poem Carl Sandburg has ever written." And in his shock, the professor erroneously concluded that Sandburg was merely a capital-T "Tough"—a poet who "hog-butchers" (this was *The Double Dealer*'s verb) and was incapable of doing anything more delicate or interesting.

Then came the May issue—which contained, incidentally, not only Wilson Jr.'s poem but the first professionally published short story by another young man who in those days still signed his name "Ernest M. Hemingway." The commentary on Sandburg this time was by Ezra Pound, writing from Paris. Pound's observations drew on a personal fact that subscribers to *The Double Dealer* might never have suspected. Pound had undergone his own experiences at the University of Pennsylvania. He enrolled at the college there, and though he completed his undergraduate work elsewhere, he returned for graduate school. And because the world is small, in his freshman year and again in graduate school he studied under—of course—Professor Schelling. Later, after Pound had left school altogether, he tried to persuade the University of Pennsylvania to grant him a Ph.D. for some of his literary studies—and Professor Schelling was the very person who turned him down. Pound kept up a friendly correspondence with his old professor, even so. In that same 1922 he alerted the professor to the existence of a not-yet published poem, *The Waste Land*. On at least one occasion Pound tried to sell the professor on Sandburg, too, in the hope of getting Sandburg a university fellowship—one more example of Pound's generous private campaign to help out the poets he admired. In *The Double Dealer*'s May 1922 issue, Pound returned to this generous campaign, and he took up the question of whether Sandburg was a Tough.

Pound observed that being a Tough was maybe not

the worst thing in the world. Literature ought to have room for people of every type, Pound argued—even journalists (this was Sandburg's actual profession) and even lumber-jacks (which was how Pound liked to think of Sandburg, though Sandburg had never been a lumberjack). Sandburg came out of Illinois. Pound was fine with that. "And Mr. Eliot was born in St. Louis." Pound did seem to understand why someone might harbor a few reservations about Sand-burg. It was just that in Pound's estimation the spectacle of a professor complaining about Sandburg's rougher edges was irritating from the outset. For what if Sandburg did lack some final sheen of culture and sophistication—whose fault was that?

Pound banged on his old drum: "Sandburg has been known for ten years, there has been plenty of time for some University to offer him a fellowship, with leisure to browse in its library and 'polish' his language. But no, de-spite the anglo-olatry of many of our 'English Depart-ments' fellowships are reserved for the docile mediocrity." And Pound launched into a general assault on an academic world that could find room neither for Carl Sandburg nor for himself.

But back to "Hog Butcher for the World" and the mys-terious question of why people used to get so excited about that line. Exactly what was Sandburg's terrible crime against propriety? A blunt industrial theme, rendered into free verse and presented in a tone of ebullient booster en-thusiasm—this was "Hog Butcher for the World" in its gist. And Sandburg, having begun that way, kept going, too:

> Tool Maker, Stacker of Wheat,
> Player with Railroads and the Nation's Freight
>   Handler

> Where was the unsettling aspect in any of that?

Walt Whitman's readers had been poring over free-verse celebrations of industrial themes for many decades by then. As for Sandburg's booster tone—why, one of the major poems in *Leaves of Grass*, "Song of the Exposition," was written on commission expressly for the purpose of cheering on the national economy, an overtly promotional enterprise from start to finish. Whitman, for a fee, recited "Song of the Exposition" aloud at a New York fair:

> Thy grapes that ripen on thy vines, the apples in thy
> orchards,
> Thy incalculable lumber, beef, pork, potatoes, thy
> coal, thy gold and silver,
> The inexhaustible iron in thy mines.
>
> All thine O sacred Union!

Lumber, beef, and even *pork*, commercially promoted in patriotic verse: these were themes so venerable as to be nineteenth century. There was another line of Whitman's too, from "A Song for Occupations," one more of his ec-statically adumbrated lists:

> The pens of live pork, the killing-hammer, the hog-
> hook, the scalder's tub, gutting, the cutter's cleaver,
> the packer's maul, and the plenteous winterwork of
> pork packing,

—all of which amounted to a grislier, fleshier tour through the slaughter-houses than anything that Sandburg ever produced, to my knowledge. Why the controversy over Sandburg, then, well into the twentieth century? The aspect that seemed so disturbingly new—what was it, exactly?

One possibility was that nothing was new. Pound recalled in *The Double Dealer* that during his years at Penn the English Department still harbored a good many doubts about Whitman. In *The Double Dealer*, having put in a word for Carl Sandburg, Pound therefore decided to put in a cautious word for Walt Whitman, too—quite as if in 1922 Whitman, and not just Sandburg, still needed a literary defense. And yet when I leaf through these disputes and controversies, it seems fairly obvious that for all the continuities from Whitman to Sandburg and the never-ending quarrels from the nineteenth century, Sandburg had, in addition, done something new that might well have taken his readers by surprise. And "Hog Butcher for the World" was precisely where he did it.

Whitman chanted the glories of the democratic masses and rapturously tabulated their many trades and occupations. But never in a million years did Walt Whitman want to sound like the democratic masses. Whitman wanted to sound like himself. He always expected that by plunging ever deeper into his own private soul, he could find his way to the larger universal soul of all existence. So downward Whitman plunged, and the deeper he delved, the statelier he became, until by the end, like a Quaker preacher or the King James Bible, he found himself exclaiming in regard to pork manufactures and other useful industries, "All thine O sacred Union!" Not that in Whitman's case this was necessarily bad.

Sandburg put on his own stately airs from time to time. In "Chicago," once he got through declaiming "Hog Butcher" and "Tool Maker" and had made his way at last to "City of the Broad Shoulders," he slowed his rhythm to a different pace altogether, and reverted to a solemn Old Testament prophetic formality:

> They tell me you are wicked and I believe them, for I
>   have seen your painted women under the gas lamps
>   luring the farm boys.

And they tell me you are crooked and I answer: Yes, it is true I have seen the gunman kill and go free to kill again.

He pictured Chicago "flinging magnetic curses," and this was grand and Whitman-like. Mostly, though, Sandburg did want to sound like the democratic masses. But instead of composing "local color" poetry in the nineteenth-century style, or affecting the quaint dialects of a rustic age, he cocked his eye and ear to the rapid-fire catch-phrases of the big-city sidewalks and billboards. He was like a photographer who arranges found objects into art—Sandburg, whose first serious job was to peddle stereopticon pictures, and who went on to marry the sister of Edward Steichen, the photographer. Only being a poet, his preferred version of a found object was an audible phrase—a found sound, so to speak. He scooped these up avidly and arrayed them across the page. This, finally, was the genuinely novel element in his early books. Sandburg wrote a "realist" poetry, but this was not just because he described social conditions. He recorded language as it was, not as it was supposed to be.

He ended "Chicago" on a trumpet blast of municipal pride, a fanfare—"proud to be Hog Butcher, Tool Maker, Stacker of Wheat," and so forth—and this was, in its fashion, magnificent. But the grandeur in these lines came from something more than venting a defiant satisfaction over industry and energy and work and everything else that prissy sensibilities might regard with horror. The grandeur here was also strictly literary—the defiant pride of a poet who had discovered in the streets a new meter and rhetoric.

There was also something more than prosodic or rhetorical in this achievement. One of Whitman's best-loved poems is a street scene called "Sparkles from the Wheel." Whitman described a knife-grinder sharpening knives on his stone wheel in front of a crowd of children, and his poem moved forward by melodically chanting its own sparkly title, and by chanting that title once again, and even a third time:

> The low hoarse purr of the whirling stone, the light-press'd blade,
> Diffusing, dropping, sideways-darting, in tiny showers of gold,
> Sparkles from the wheel.

The poem had a charm, yet it hinted at something deeper, too. Whitman in that poem presented himself as a phantom within the crowd, gazing on the scene as if from some other world, and this makes you feel that you, too, are standing somewhere in the zone of the spirit, wide-eyed and observant—agog at the possibility of an altogether different universe.

Sandburg wrote his own version of this poem, using his own theme of manual labor and a roughly similar melodic structure of repeated phrases and internal rhymes, and he even threw in a few sparkles, though he called them "flashes." This was Sandburg's "Manual System," about a telephone operator in the days when women operators sat in front of vast consoles, plugging wires:

> Mary has a thingamajig clamped on her ears
> And sits all day taking plugs out and sticking plugs in.
> Flashes and flashes—voices and voices
>   calling for ears to pour words in
> Faces at the ends of wires asking for other faces
>   at the ends of other wires:
> All day taking plugs out and sticking plugs in,
> Mary has a thingamajig clamped on her ears.

Only how much lighter is Sandburg's poem! How jaunty!—and how different, on a philosophical level. Nothing mysterious haunts "Manual System"—not one hint of an alternative universe, not one suggestion that Carl Sandburg is a figure from the world of the spirit. There is merely that entertaining word "thingamajig"—the word that captures all your attention. Instead of the truer universe that lurks behind whatever stands before us, there is merely the ordinary hubbub of modern life, with its funny neologisms. Instead of a mysterious depth, an audible surface.

The search for the catch-phrases of the spoken language, the effort to create a poetry that doesn't bubble up from the mystic soul but precipitates instead from already-existing sounds and phrases, the suggestion that language and not the unseen universe should occupy our attention —this is what Sandburg shared with Ezra Pound. When Pound sat down to write, he wanted to conjure a gigantic universe of language—a poetic language that was indiscriminately Anglo-Saxon, Greek, Latin, Chinese, and half a dozen other things. Pound wanted to leave the impression that in composing verse he was not reaching down into his ecstatic soul—he was merely collecting phrases and entire poems from the universal language that he found on the library shelves and sometimes on the streets, all of which he set about transcribing with exquisite technical skill.

Pound ornamented his pages with Greek letters and Chinese calligraphy to render his notion of a universal language still more vivid. Sandburg filled his own pages with capital-letter slogans that seemed to have come directly from the commercial billboards. But something in those two approaches expressed the same idea. It was the shared notion that to write is to quote; that there is no inner soul that can be tapped and sounded; there is only language, which is already speaking, and we have only to open our eyes and ears.

Sandburg, for his part, identified intensely with Pound. The poem "Chicago" appeared in *Poetry* magazine in the city of Chicago, and Pound, too, contributed to that magazine. In 1916, when Sandburg was 38, he published an essay on Pound in those same pages, and his enthusiasm seemed boundless. Pound, he said, was "the best man writing poetry today." Does this seem odd or hard to understand—an aw-shucks man of the people like Sandburg paying extravagant homage to an abrasive aristocrat of letters like Pound? But Sandburg in those days was distinctly under Pound's influence, and the more he drew from Pound, the more faithfully he remained a man of the people. In his *Poetry* essay, Sandburg quoted in full a poem by Pound called "On His Own Face in a Glass":

O strange face there in the glass!

O ribald company, O saintly host!
O sorrow-swept my fool,

What answer?
O ye myriad
That strive and play and pass,
Jest, challenge, counterlie,
I   ?   I   ?   I   ?
And ye?

The eight lines in that poem seem to have been scooped up from Shakespeare's time, even if the poet also makes a show of his own modernity by fooling around with question marks. And this, too, became an inspiration for Sandburg. He produced his own eight lines, using language that he, too, seemed to scoop up from some other place than his own mysterious soul. Only in Sandburg's case, this other place appeared to be the easy vernacular of the checkout counter:

Phizzog

This face you got,
This here phizzog you carry around,
You never picked it out for yourself,
    at all, at all—did you?
This here phizzog—somebody handed it
    to you—am I right?
Somebody said, "Here's yours, now go see
    what you can do with it."
Somebody slipped it to you and it was like
    a package marked:
"No goods exchanged after being taken away"—
This face you got.

Sandburg was not a big thinker, and was at his gassiest when he pretended to be. The treasures of a dozen literatures and a thousand technical skills did not lie before him on his writing table the way they did for Ezra Pound. But even if Sandburg could never have given a lucid theoretical explanation of his every turn of phrase, this early poetry of his did manage to hit a note that was wonderfully fresh. His genius consisted mostly of presenting that fresh and up-to-date sound in a style almost obnoxiously noisy, like a radio turned up too loud—an aggressive act that might well have annoyed or even shocked some readers. In the world of poetry, a line like "Hog Butcher for the World" was, after all, *news*, but did he have to blare it quite so loudly? He kept on blaring. And guess what? His news has stayed news.

"Chicago" departed from Whitman's path in still another way, and this had to do with ideas about history and society. In *Leaves of Grass* Whitman wanted to paint a panorama of American life, which meant that each of his poems, the masterpieces and non-masterpieces alike, made its contribution, and everything fit together, and the panorama grew larger by the page. Sandburg adopted something of that same principle in composing his poems about Chicago and the industrial Midwest—not just in *Chicago Poems* but in big portions of all of his main verse collections. The individual snapshots that he included, miniatures like "Hangman" and "Dynamiter," ought to be seen as faces in his larger picture, and the context gives those miniatures a pathos and drama that otherwise might not be theirs.

Whitman entertained a very peculiar idea about good and evil and America, though. He pictured good as eternal and real, and evil as a passing element that was ultimately going to yield to the good. This was a Christian idea, in its origins, but Whitman gave the idea a patriotic twist, and he presented as his Christ-figure Abraham Lincoln, the Redeemer-President, whose death, as Whitman describes it, is an evil that nonetheless contributes to the ultimate re-demption of America and of mankind. Sandburg felt an in-stinctive attraction to a few aspects of this same idea—or at least sometimes he did. That was why in "Chicago," after proclaiming Chicago's industrial greatness and weeping over Chicago's prostitution, corruption, and murders, he returned at the end to a new and still more vigorous decla-ration of how marvelous and grand and creative was the whole shebang. The evils were evil, yes; but they figured in a larger something, which was good.

But mostly Sandburg took his own tack on good and evil and America. He was optimistic about American life, and he was pessimistic, and he separated each of those moods from the other, and he indulged them both, until his optimism was wildly enthusiastic, and his pessimism was bleak and bitter, and nothing seemed to tie the one impulse to the other. And this peculiar combination of sentiments, as much as the prosodic billboard adventure of "Hog Butcher for the World," finally marked Sandburg as a man of his own time, and not of Whitman's. Or maybe Sandburg's combination of deep optimism and infuriated bitterness was specifically a Chicago attitude from those years. You see a version of that same double emotion in Theodore Dreiser's Chicago novels—Dreiser, who shared with Sandburg a poetic ear for the language of the immigrant streets—and in the novels of Upton Sinclair, whose *The Jungle*, from 1906, had already given Chicago meatpacking a universal notoriety. Then again the optimism-pessimism combination was in those years a political attitude as well, and it found its Chicago home in one very distinctive organization, whose name was the Socialist Party.

The Socialist Party was never a gigantic enterprise in the United States. But in the first couple of decades of the twentieth century, the party did succeed in dominating some rural districts and a number of big-city neighborhoods and quite a few trade unions. It ruled the roost in Milwaukee and a few other middle-sized cities, and it did have its national politicians and a popular press. The party's rank-and-file supporters tended to be immigrant workers and their children—the kind of people whose political memories traced back to the Social Democrats of Germany or Eastern Europe or the Nordic countries. Yet for all of its immigrant cultures and foreign languages, America's Socialist Party was genuinely American, and the party's instinct for optimism-pessimism drew on memories of the Civil War and the American past as well as on the realities of turn-of-the-century industrial life. A Lincoln-mania figured in the Socialist lore, too, and this was triply so in Illinois, the land of Lincoln.

Sandburg was himself the son of Swedish immigrants. He grew up in Galesburg, Illinois, volunteered for the Spanish-American War in a unit from Illinois, and mostly sat out the war in Puerto Rico—all of which made him a pretty typical recruit for the Socialist movement. After he was done with peddling stereopticon pictures, the Social-ists offered him a living, too, and hired him as a party or-ganizer in Wisconsin. He contributed articles to the Mil-waukee Socialist newspapers. He became the secretary to Milwaukee's Socialist mayor. In those days Sandburg could reasonably be described as, to use the old political lan-guage, a "right-wing" Socialist. This meant an old-school European-style social democrat, cautious and plodding. Or to put it more colorfully but just as authentically, Sand-burg was a "sewer socialist"—the kind of social democrat who worried more about improving municipal services than about achieving the workers' paradise. That was the Wisconsin style.

In 1912, though, he moved to Chicago and began writing for the mainstream Chicago press, and he evolved into a "left-wing" Socialist, or what was called, just as au-thentically, an "impossibilist." He sent his poems and his essay on Pound to *Poetry* magazine, but he also sent "Billy Sunday" (or in its toned-down version, "To a Contempo-rary Bunkshooter") and other poems to Chicago's impossi-bilist journal, the *International Socialist Review*. Sandburg cranked out monthly journalism for the *International So-cialist Review*, and he kept doing this until by mid-1915 he had become the magazine's star contributor, sometimes publishing labor reportage under his own name, some-times under the name of "Jack Phillips" or "Militant," sometimes contributing poems under his own byline or under the initials C.S.—and typically appearing twice or even three times per issue. Upton Sinclair's byline used to appear in that magazine too, and Jack London's. But Sandburg dominated the pages.

The Chicago *International Socialist Review* had a sister magazine in New York, *The Masses*, and of those two magazines the *International Socialist Review* was less witty and less beautifully designed. But it was also less corny. Both magazines, in any case, managed to be vigorous and imaginative—a quality that came from Sandburg's Chicago reportage and from John Reed's New York reportage, from the poetry and the Ash-Can draughtsmen, and sometimes from the political theory, which in both magazines leaned so far to the left as to veer out of conventional social democracy altogether. Both of those magazines ended up falling slightly in love with the Wobblies, or Industrial Workers of the World, on the far left of the labor movement— America's revolutionary syndicalists, whose impossibilism was exceptionally impossible.

The *International Socialist Review* published essays by Anton Pannekoek and other writers from the Dutch ultra-left, as well, and these doctrines somehow took root in Chicago's Bohemia, the Dill Pickle Club (and got picked up from there and disseminated to later generations by Kenneth Rexroth and others). And all of these features of the magazine, its politics, its poetry, the drawings and cartoons, the memories of the Civil War and of Lincoln, the dispatches from European theorists—all of this harmonized perfectly with the extravagant optimism-pessimism of the Chicago novelists and of Sandburg's poetry: the fecund, bifurcated, fragile mood of those years. Then came World War I.

The war rattled Sandburg pretty badly. His early

attitude was pacifist indignation, and this attitude fit into the Socialist Party's official position and even into its unofficial position, especially in places like Milwaukee and Chicago where German immigrants played a big role in the party. Sandburg's anti-war poems tended to be a little shrill. But the war took an unexpected turn, and so did Sandburg's thinking. Early in 1917 the Russian Revolution overthrew the tsar, and for most of the next year liberal democrats in Russia stood at the head of the new government, until the Bolsheviks shoved them aside—and even then no one really knew who were those Russian Bolsheviks or what they wanted, which allowed people all over the world to fantasize about the Bolshevik idea. And as these events took place in far-away Europe, Woodrow Wilson's notion of a war for democracy began to look ever more attractive.

President Wilson brought America into the war with that idea in mind. The democratic republics of the world, Russia's brand-new one included, did appear to be united against the German kaiser and perhaps even against the very principle of authoritarian government. And Sandburg found himself in a terrible fix, with each bifurcated half of his impossible optimism-pessimism pulling in a different direction—the optimism pulling him toward patriotic solidarity with President Wilson's war for democracy, the pessimism pulling him into ever more anger and bitterness and into an eager search for new political alternatives.

The Socialist Party stuck to its anti-war position even after Wilson decided on war. A little committee of old-time Socialists nonetheless came out in favor of Wilson's policy, conspired a bit with the Wilson administration, and set out to agitate for support in the labor movement and on the left. These people were, in the parlance of the day, neither sewer Socialists nor impossibilist Socialists. These people were "State Department Socialists." Sandburg became a State Department Socialist—which by the way was not at all unusual among the left-wing writers and intellectuals. He went to work for the pro-war committee. He must have been a genuine asset, too—a radical journalist with a popular touch and an avant-garde panache. Yet even after signing up with the pro-war committee, Sandburg never lost his sympathy for the revolutionary left. President Wilson was a champion of democracy abroad and of labor reforms at home, but as is sometimes forgotten, he also presided over a fairly systematic repression of his political opponents. Mass arrests broke up the anti-war Socialists. The Wobbly leaders were thrown in jail. And this was not at all to Sandburg's taste.

And so even while toiling on behalf of the pro-war committee, he cranked out journalism defending the persecuted Wobblies against the accusation that labeled them as anti-war. This was not entirely honest or straightforward on Sandburg's part. The Wobblies were, in fact, anti-war. But what the hell, each of Sandburg's multiple bylines appeared to have acquired its own personality in those years. There were moments when the patriotic journalist "Carl Sandburg" was cranking out propaganda for the pro-war Socialists, and the pseudonymous ultra-radical journalist "Jack Phillips" was cranking out propaganda for the Wobblies, and "Sandburg" sometimes favored the war and the Wobblies at the same time. The man was confused. And things got worse.

In 1918 the Scripps news service in Chicago dispatched him to Stockholm to report on events in northern Europe, and Sandburg, who had never seen his ancestral Scandinavia, took up his new post. He struck up a friendly relationship in Stockholm with an old Chicago immigrant radical who had returned to Russia and had become an agent of the Bolsheviks. Sandburg set out to aid the Bolsheviks, just as he had aided the Wobblies back home. After seven weeks in Stockholm, he returned to the United States, bearing with him a "Letter to American Workingmen" by Lenin, the purpose of which was to help bring into existence a Communist Party in the United States—a new organization loyal to the new Soviet Union and to Lenin himself.

Theodore Draper, the greatest of the historians of American Communism, long ago presented Sandburg's transmission of this document as a seminal event in the history of the American left. But according to Philip R. Yannella, one of Sandburg's biographers, the Bolsheviks relied on more than one courier and someone else had already smuggled Lenin's letter into the United States. In any event, Sandburg also brought with him $10,000 in Bolshevik cash to deliver to a Finnish-American Socialist organization that was expected to line up with the new Communists. Not too surprisingly, when Sandburg arrived in New York on the ship from Stockholm on Christmas Day 1918, he was greeted, in Yannella's summary, "by agents representing Military Intelligence, the Department of Justice, the Bureau of Investigation, United States Customs, and the New York State attorney general," all of whom took an interest in the $10,000.

Sandburg survived the inquiries that followed, though he seems never to have fully acknowledged what he was doing with the Bolshevik cash. (Perhaps it was a coincidence, but in that same 1918 he published *Cornhuskers*, with its ruefully humorous poem "Lawyer," about a lawyer preparing an appeal for a convicted defendant—"speaking in a soft voice, speaking in a voice slightly colored with bitter wrongs mingled with monumental patience, speaking with mythic Atlas shoulders of many preposterous, unjust circumstances.") It was certainly the case that Sandburg in those years cut a ridiculous figure. Apart from "Lawyer," *Cornhuskers* contained pro-war poems and anti-war poems alike—and both sets of poems were written in the same unattractive tone of jeering hysteria. The pro-war poems are harder to swallow. A simple-minded anti-war jeer may be naïve, perhaps objectionably so; but a simple-minded pro-war jeer always seems a little mad. In "The Four Brothers" Sandburg wrote:

> Eating to kill,
> Sleeping to kill,
> Asked by their mothers to kill,
> Wished by four-fifths of the world to kill—
> To cut the kaiser's throat,
> To hack the kaiser's head,
> To hang the kaiser on a high-horizon gibbet.

Only this poem, instead of being an anti-war satire, was in fact a pro-war recruiting poem!—which I have mercifully omitted from the present anthology.

I have to say, though, something about Sandburg's confusions from those days seems to me humanly understandable and even likeable. He wanted to cling to his socialist ideals, and this was reasonable, given the industrial conditions. He wanted to stand by his persecuted old friends from the Wobblies, even if he didn't approve anymore of their every position. He wanted to believe in the democratic war goals of Woodrow Wilson. He hoped that Lenin's Bolshevism would turn out to be a good thing. He did not want to abandon the optimism-pessimism of his pre-war imagination. He wanted to be a good American without ceasing to be well-loved by America's impossibilists and syndicalists. Every one of those urges seems to me comprehensible in the context of the time. Nor did these confusions stand in the way of writing good poetry. The years when Sandburg was sunk into his deepest befuddlement on political questions were also years in which he stood at the height of his artistic powers—the years of *Chicago Poems* (1916), *Cornhuskers* (1918), and *Smoke and Steel* (1920), his three finest collections.

He couldn't go on like this forever, though. Confusion can be commendable, but only for so long. The pre-war Socialists with their marvelous optimism-pessimism survived the war only as a shell of their no-longer ebullient selves. The syndicalists virtually disappeared. The followers of Lenin became the big energetic force on the American left for the next few decades. But Communism had no appeal to Sandburg once he had taken a serious look. What to do, then? In 1922, the year of *The Double Dealer* discussion, the year of *The Waste Land*, Sandburg wrote a humorous children's book, *Rootabaga Stories*, about a girl named Ax Me No Questions and other characters, and this was a good thing to do. But maybe the children's book signified that for the moment having lost the desire to ax any more questions, he wanted to pull back from his old impulse to stand at the far edge of modern thought. So he pulled back, and ruminated, and after a while he came up with a new project. This was to throw himself back into the nineteenth-century pathways of Walt Whitman and to write a biography of Lincoln, on a gigantic scale.

The six volumes that resulted, *Abraham Lincoln: The Prairie Years* (two volumes) and *The War Years* (four volumes) have acquired a bad reputation largely because of a remark by Edmund Wilson: "The cruelest thing that has happened to Lincoln since he was shot by Booth was to fall into the hands of Carl Sandburg." The remark is not without justice in regard to *The Prairie Years*, Volume One, and perhaps Volume Two as well—those early volumes with their hundreds of pages of corn-pone storytelling, written as if for the readers of *Rootabaga Stories* at a slightly older age. But *The War Years* is something else, which Edmund Wilson failed to see. Wilson, it ought to be remembered, underwent his own period of political befuddlement, which led him to conclude that Lincoln was a tyrant and the Confederates had a point. This at least was never Sandburg's error.

I am in no position to judge the giant biography on scholarly grounds. A proper Lincoln expert ought to come along someday and annotate a modern edition, informing us about the ways in which Sandburg's portrait hit the mark, and the ways in which his research and thinking have been superseded. But I do see that in the four volumes of *The War Years* Sandburg adopted a harder-edged, more factual tone, and he composed his biography with an appreciative eye for the poetry and song lyrics of the time. Some lingering remnant of his old socialism clung to his analysis too. Sandburg in the final volume put the freeing of the slaves at the center of his story, which Edmund Wilson in his own account of the Civil War never managed to do. Sandburg saw in Emancipation a social revolution—a defeat for the planter class and a rise to heroism of vast masses of militant ex-slaves. Walt Whitman plays a surprisingly small role in Sandburg's *Lincoln*, yet when he does at last appear, Sandburg quotes him at length on the death of the Redeemer-President. And your heart pounds.

The Lincoln biography succeeded too in straightening out Sandburg's political confusions. Now he knew exactly where he stood. He was an American nationalist on liberal and democratic grounds, not averse to plucking a sentimental string for hours at a time. Whether this newly clarified posture did his poetry any good is a question. Clarity and poetry are not the same. But this may merely suggest that in choosing to spend more of his energy in the later 1920s and '30s on composing his giant biography than on writing poetry, Sandburg had judged himself correctly —not that he didn't go on to write *The People, Yes*, which has its passable moments, and other poems.

One of the oddities of Sandburg's later career is how faithfully it ran parallel to Ezra Pound's, except with each man inverting the other's experiences, as in a mirror. Sandburg lapsed into his Lincoln-mania and his American nationalism, and Pound took up the weird joint cult of Jefferson and Mussolini, which made him a fascist. Sandburg during World War II delivered patriotic radio addresses on behalf of Franklin Roosevelt and the anti-fascist effort. Pound during World War II, from his exile's home in Italy, delivered anti-Semitic radio addresses on behalf of Mussolini.

In 1945 the American military in Italy locked up Pound and brought him back to the United States and charged him, all too justly, with treason. Sandburg in that same decade was awarded the Pulitzer Prize for his *Lincoln* and in 1951 was awarded the same prize for his *Complete Poems*. He was decorated with honorary degrees from universities too—now that in his years of success he no longer needed academic degrees. Only this kind of personal triumph ended up wreaking the same disastrous effect on Sandburg's reputation, in the eyes of the literary world, as arrest and disgrace did on Ezra Pound's—a devastating blow to each man's personal prestige. Pound was consigned to a federal insane asylum in Washington, D.C. Sandburg for his part was invited in 1959 to address a joint session of Congress—though, as someone once remarked, Sandburg was at least allowed to leave after he had completed his speech.

Pound's thirteen years in the asylum made him famous, though largely as a fascist and a traitor. Sandburg became even more of a celebrity—though mostly as a patriot. His face appeared on the cover of *Time* magazine. Pound wrote poems about roving troubadours. Sandburg became one. He toured the country, playing guitar and singing—though this represented Sandburg at his most charming, as even Edmund Wilson had to acknowledge. Pound's writings in later years became ever harder to read, until whole sections of his poetry ended up pretty much incomprehensible. Sandburg's poetry likewise became hard to read, not because he was incomprehensible but because he seemed so damn corny and simple-minded.

Yet it is moving to learn that Sandburg and Pound never did entirely give up their ancient friendship—even if in later years friendship had to make allowances for the twists and turns of personal destiny. Sandburg was not entirely averse to the notion that Pound, his "crazy brudder," ought to be locked up. Sandburg's biographer Penelope Niven quotes him saying, "It won't hurt Ezra to do a little time." That was in 1950, when Pound had already done a lot of time. Yet, even then, Sandburg insisted that he intended to go on reading Pound, the poet. Pound himself responded by inviting Sandburg to visit him in the asylum. A few years later a group of distinguished writers made a public call for Pound to be released, and Sandburg's name was associated with the group. He went on affirming his personal loyalty as well. "I'll read the sonofabitch as long as I live," said America's most famously patriotic poet about America's most famous literary traitor—in a remark that was picked up by a comedian's tape recorder during the preparation for Sandburg's appearance on the Milton Berle show. And all of this made perfect sense.

Sandburg the poet was a man of the 1910s and '20s. He was faithful to his friends and alliances of that long-ago era because he was faithful to himself, and this was the proper thing to be. He had a knack for hitting the right note in those long-ago years, and whenever he did this, which was often enough, his note sounded supremely modern at the time, and some of those notes have continued to sound that way, in solid demonstration of the purity of his achievement. "Phizzog"—that word was genius. "No goods exchanged after being taken away"—an undeniable truth. "Thingamajig"—a poem in itself. And "Hog Butcher for the World"—a line from 1914 that, even now, with its heavily aspirated H, causes in the reader strange and unpredictable intakes and expulsions of breath, a line that has always been partly defiant, partly humorous, and partly a five-word, unforgettable manifesto for a new poetry.

Paul Berman
2006

Chicago

Hog Butcher for the World,
Tool Maker, Stacker of Wheat,
Player with Railroads and the Nation's Freight
    Handler;
Stormy, husky, brawling,
City of the Big Shoulders:

They tell me you are wicked and I believe them, for I
    have seen your painted women under the gas lamps
    luring the farm boys.
And they tell me you are crooked and I answer: Yes, it is
    true I have seen the gunman kill and go free to kill
    again.
And they tell me you are brutal and my reply is: On the
    faces of women and children I have seen the marks
    of wanton hunger.
And having answered so I turn once more to those who
    sneer at this my city, and I give them back the sneer
    and say to them:
Come and show me another city with lifted head singing
    so proud to be alive and coarse and strong and
    cunning.

Flinging magnetic curses amid the toil of piling job on
      job, here is a tall bold slugger set vivid against the
      little soft cities;

Fierce as a dog with tongue lapping for action, cunning
      as a savage pitted against the wilderness,

          Bareheaded,

          Shoveling,

          Wrecking,

          Planning,

          Building, breaking, rebuilding,

Under the smoke, dust all over his mouth, laughing with
      white teeth,

Under the terrible burden of destiny laughing as a young
      man laughs,

Laughing even as an ignorant fighter laughs who has
      never lost a battle,

Bragging and laughing that under his wrist is the pulse,
      and under his ribs the heart of the people,

                Laughing!

Laughing the stormy, husky, brawling laughter of Youth,
      half-naked, sweating, proud to be Hog Butcher,
      Tool Maker, Stacker of Wheat, Player with Rail-
      roads and Freight Handler to the Nation.

Masses

Among the mountains I wandered and saw blue haze and
      red crag and was amazed;

On the beach where the long push under the endless tide
      maneuvers, I stood silent;

Under the stars on the prairie watching the Dipper slant
over the horizon's grass, I was full of thoughts.
Great men, pageants of war and labor, soldiers and
workers, mothers lifting their children—these all I
touched, and felt the solemn thrill of them.
And then one day I got a true look at the Poor, millions of
the Poor, patient and toiling; more patient than crags,
tides, and stars; innumerable, patient as the darkness
of night—and all broken, humble ruins of nations.

Lost

Desolate and lone
All night long on the lake
Where fog trails and mist creeps,
The whistle of a boat
Calls and cries unendingly,
Like some lost child
In tears and trouble
Hunting the harbor's breast
And the harbor's eyes.

The Harbor

Passing through huddled and ugly walls
By doorways where women
Looked from their hunger-deep eyes,
Haunted with shadows of hunger-hands.

Out from the huddled and ugly walls,
I came sudden, at the city's edge,
On a blue burst of lake,
Long lake waves breaking under the sun
On a spray-flung curve of shore;
And a fluttering storm of gulls,
Masses of great gray wings
And flying white bellies
Veering and wheeling free in the open.

They Will Say

Of my city the worst that men will ever say is this:
You took little children away from the sun and the dew,
And the glimmers that played in the grass under the
    great sky,
And the reckless rain; you put them between walls
To work, broken and smothered, for bread and wages,
To eat dust in their throats and die empty-hearted
For a little handful of pay on a few Saturday nights.

Mill-Doors

You never come back.
I say good-by when I see you going in the doors,
The hopeless open doors that call and wait
And take you then for—how many cents a day?
How many cents for the sleepy eyes and fingers?

I say good-by because I know they tap your wrists,
In the dark, in the silence, day by day,
And all the blood of you drop by drop,
And you are old before you are young.
    You never come back.

A Teamster's Farewell

Sobs En Route to a Penitentiary

Good-by now to the streets and the clash of wheels and
    locking hubs,
The sun coming on the brass buckles and harness knobs,
The muscles of the horses sliding under their heavy
    haunches,
Good-by now to the traffic policeman and his whistle,
The smash of the iron hoof on the stones,
All the crazy wonderful slamming roar of the street—
O God, there's noises I'm going to be hungry for.

Fish Crier

I know a Jew fish crier down on Maxwell Street with a
    voice like a north wind blowing over corn stubble in
    January.
He dangles herring before prospective customers evinc-
    ing a joy identical with that of Pavlowa dancing.

His face is that of a man terribly glad to be selling fish, terribly glad that God made fish, and customers to whom he may call his wares from a pushcart.

Picnic Boat

Sunday night and the park policemen tell each other it is dark as a stack of black cats on Lake Michigan.
A big picnic boat comes home to Chicago from the peach farms of Saugatuck.
Hundreds of electric bulbs break the night's darkness, a flock of red and yellow birds with wings at a standstill.
Running along the deck railings are festoons and leaping in curves are loops of light from prow and stern to the tall smokestacks.
Over the hoarse crunch of waves at my pier comes a hoarse answer in the rhythmic oompa of the brasses playing a Polish folk-song for the home-comers.

Muckers

Twenty men stand watching the muckers.
    Stabbing the sides of the ditch
    Where clay gleams yellow,
    Driving the blades of their shovels

Deeper and deeper for the new gas mains,
Wiping sweat off their faces
With red bandanas.
The muckers work on . . pausing . . to pull
Their boots out of suckholes where they slosh.

Of the twenty looking on
Ten murmur, "O, it's a hell of a job,"
Ten others, "Jesus, I wish I had the job."

Blacklisted

Why shall I keep the old name?
What is a name anywhere anyway?
A name is a cheap thing all fathers and mothers leave
    each child:
A job is a job and I want to live, so
Why does God Almighty or anybody else care whether I
    take a new name to go by?

Mag

I wish to God I never saw you, Mag.
I wish you never quit your job and came along with me.
I wish we never bought a license and a white dress
For you to get married in the day we ran off to a
    minister

And told him we would love each other and take care of
     each other
Always and always long as the sun and the rain lasts
     anywhere.
Yes, I'm wishing now you lived somewhere away from
     here
And I was a bum on the bumpers a thousand miles away
     dead broke.
      I wish the kids had never come
      And rent and coal and clothes to pay for
      And a grocery man calling for cash,
      Every day cash for beans and prunes.
      I wish to God I never saw you, Mag.
      I wish to God the kids had never come.

Anna Imroth

Cross the hands over the breast here—so.
Straighten the legs a little more—so.
And call for the wagon to come and take her home.
Her mother will cry some and so will her sisters and
     brothers.
But all of the others got down and they are safe and this is
     the only one of the factory girls who wasn't lucky in
     making the jump when the fire broke.
It is the hand of God and the lack of fire escapes.

Mamie

Mamie beat her head against the bars of a little Indiana
   town and dreamed of romance and big things off
   somewhere the way the railroad trains all ran.

She could see the smoke of the engines get lost down
   where the streaks of steel flashed in the sun and
   when the newspapers came in on the morning mail
   she knew there was a big Chicago far off, where all
   the trains ran.

She got tired of the barber shop boys and the post office
   chatter and the church gossip and the old pieces the
   band played on the Fourth of July and Decoration
   Day

And sobbed at her fate and beat her head against the bars
   and was going to kill herself

When the thought came to her that if she was going to
   die she might as well die struggling for a clutch of
   romance among the streets of Chicago.

She has a job now at six dollars a week in the basement of
   the Boston Store

And even now she beats her head against the bars in the
   same old way and wonders if there is a bigger place
   the railroads run to from Chicago where maybe
   there is

> romance
> and big things
> and real dreams
> that never go smash.

Personality

Musings of a Police Reporter in the Identification Bureau

You have loved forty women, but you have only one
   thumb.
You have led a hundred secret lives, but you mark only
   one thumb.
You go round the world and fight in a thousand wars and
   win all the world's honors, but when you come back
   home the print of the one thumb your mother gave
   you is the same print of thumb you had in the old
   home when your mother kissed you and said
   good-by.
Out of the whirling womb of time come millions of men
   and their feet crowd the earth and they cut one an-
   other's throats for room to stand and among them all
   are not two thumbs alike.
Somewhere is a Great God of Thumbs who can tell the
   inside story of this.

Cumulatives

Storms have beaten on this point of land
And ships gone to wreck here
            and the passers-by remember it
            with talk on the deck at night
            as they near it.

Fists have beaten on the face of this old prize-fighter
And his battles have held the sporting pages
and on the street they indicate him with their
right fore-finger as one who once wore
a championship belt.

A hundred stories have been published and a thousand
rumored
About why this tall dark man has divorced two beautiful
young women
And married a third who resembles the first two
and they shake their heads and say, "There he
goes,"
when he passes by in sunny weather or in rain
along the city streets.

To Certain Journeymen

Undertakers, hearse drivers, grave diggers,
I speak to you as one not afraid of your business.

You handle dust going to a long country,
You know the secret behind your job is the same whether
you lower the coffin with modern, automatic ma-
chinery, well-oiled and noiseless, or whether the
body is laid in by naked hands and then covered by
the shovels.

Your day's work is done with laughter many days of the
    year,
And you earn a living by those who say good-by today in
    thin whispers.

Limited

I am riding on a limited express, one of the crack trains of
    the nation.
Hurtling across the prairie into blue haze and dark air go
    fifteen all-steel coaches holding a thousand people.
(All the coaches shall be scrap and rust and all the men
    and women laughing in the diners and sleepers shall
    pass to ashes.)
I ask a man in the smoker where he is going and he an-
    swers: "Omaha."

A Coin

Your western heads here cast on money,
You are the two that fade away together,
            Partners in the mist.

            Lunging buffalo shoulder,
            Lean Indian face,
We who come after where you are gone
Salute your forms on the new nickel.

You are
To us:
The past.

Runners
On the prairie:
Good-by.

Dynamiter

I sat with a dynamiter at supper in a German saloon
    eating steak and onions.
And he laughed and told stories of his wife and children
    and the cause of labor and the working class.
It was laughter of an unshakable man knowing life to be a
    rich and red-blooded thing.
Yes, his laugh rang like the call of gray birds filled with a
    glory of joy ramming their winged flight through a
    rain storm.
His name was in many newspapers as an enemy of the
    nation and few keepers of churches or schools would
    open their doors to him.
Over the steak and onions not a word was said of his deep
    days and nights as a dynamiter.
Only I always remember him as a lover of life, a lover of
    children, a lover of all free, reckless laughter every-
    where—lover of red hearts and red blood the world
    over.

Ice Handler

I know an ice handler who wears a flannel shirt with pearl
buttons the size of a dollar,
And he lugs a hundred-pound hunk into a saloon ice-box,
helps himself to cold ham and rye bread,
Tells the bartender it's hotter than yesterday and will be
hotter yet to-morrow, by Jesus,
And is on his way with his head in the air and a hard pair
of fists.
He spends a dollar or so every Saturday night on a two
hundred pound woman who washes dishes in the
Hotel Morrison.
He remembers when the union was organized he broke
the noses of two scabs and loosened the nuts so the
wheels came off six different wagons one morning,
and he came around and watched the ice melt in the
street.
All he was sorry for was one of the scabs bit him on the
knuckles of the right hand so they bled when he
came around to the saloon to tell the boys about it.

Jack

Jack was a swarthy, swaggering son-of-a-gun.
He worked thirty years on the railroad, ten hours a day,
and his hands were tougher than sole leather.

He married a tough woman and they had eight children
and the woman died and the children grew up and
went away and wrote the old man every two years.

He died in the poorhouse sitting on a bench in the sun
telling reminiscences to other old men whose women
were dead and children scattered.

There was joy on his face when he died as there was joy
on his face when he lived—he was a swarthy, swag-
gering son-of-a-gun.

Under a Hat Rim

While the hum and the hurry
Of passing footfalls
Beat in my ear like the restless surf
Of a wind-blown sea,
A soul came to me
Out of the look on a face.

Eyes like a lake
Where a storm-wind roams
Caught me from under
The rim of a hat.
I thought of a midsea wreck
and bruised fingers clinging
to a broken state-room door.

In a Breath

To the Williamson Brothers

High noon. White sun flashes on the Michigan Avenue asphalt. Drum of hoofs and whirr of motors. Women trapesing along in flimsy clothes catching play of sun-fire to their skin and eyes.

Inside the playhouse are movies from under the sea. From the heat of pavements and the dust of sidewalks, passers-by go in a breath to be witnesses of large cool sponges, large cool fishes, large cool valleys and ridges of coral spread silent in the soak of the ocean floor thousands of years.

A naked swimmer dives. A knife in his right hand shoots a streak at the throat of a shark. The tail of the shark lashes. One swing would kill the swimmer. . . Soon the knife goes into the soft under-neck of the veering fish. . . Its mouthful of teeth, each tooth a dagger itself, set row on row, glistens when the shuddering, yawning cadaver is hauled up by the brothers of the swimmer.

Outside in the street is the murmur and singing of life in the sun—horses, motors, women trapesing along in flimsy clothes, play of sun-fire in their blood.

Bronzes

I

The bronze General Grant riding a bronze horse in
    Lincoln Park
Shrivels in the sun by day when the motor cars whirr by
    in long processions going somewhere to keep ap-
    pointment for dinner and matineés and buying and
    selling
Though in the dusk and nightfall when high waves are
    piling
On the slabs of the promenade along the lake shore near
    by
I have seen the general dare the combers come closer
And make to ride his bronze horse out into the hoofs and
    guns of the storm.

II

I cross Lincoln Park on a winter night when the snow is
    falling.
Lincoln in bronze stands among the white lines of snow,
    his bronze forehead meeting soft echoes of the
    newsies crying forty thousand men are dead along
    the Yser, his bronze ears listening to the mumbled
    roar of the city at his bronze feet.
A lithe Indian on a bronze pony, Shakespeare seated with
    long legs in bronze, Garibaldi in a bronze cape, they
    hold places in the cold, lonely snow to-night on
    their pedestals and so they will hold them past mid-
    night and into the dawn.

Ready to Kill

Ten minutes now I have been looking at this.
I have gone by here before and wondered about it.
This is a bronze memorial of a famous general
Riding horseback with a flag and a sword and a revolver
     on him.
I want to smash the whole thing into a pile of junk to be
     hauled away to the scrap yard.
I put it straight to you,
After the farmer, the miner, the shop man, the factory
     hand, the fireman and the teamster,
Have all been remembered with bronze memorials,
Shaping them on the job of getting all of us
Something to eat and something to wear,
When they stack a few silhouettes
          Against the sky
          Here in the park,
And show the real huskies that are doing the work of the
     world, and feeding people instead of butchering
     them,
Then maybe I will stand here
And look easy at this general of the army holding a flag in
     the air,
And riding like hell on horseback
Ready to kill anybody that gets in his way,
Ready to run the red blood and slush the bowels of men
     all over the sweet new grass of the prairie.

Skyscraper

By day the skyscraper looms in the smoke and sun and has a soul.

Prairie and valley, streets of the city, pour people into it and they mingle among its twenty floors and are poured out again back to the streets, prairies and valleys.

It is the men and women, boys and girls so poured in and out all day that give the building a soul of dreams and thoughts and memories.

(Dumped in the sea or fixed in a desert, who would care for the building or speak its name or ask a policeman the way to it?)

Elevators slide on their cables and tubes catch letters and parcels and iron pipes carry gas and water in and sewage out.

Wires climb with secrets, carry light and carry words, and tell terrors and profits and loves—curses of men grappling plans of business and questions of women in plots of love.

Hour by hour the caissons reach down to the rock of the earth and hold the building to a turning planet.

Hour by hour the girders play as ribs and reach out and hold together the stone walls and floors.

Hour by hour the hand of the mason and the stuff of the mortar clinch the pieces and parts to the shape an architect voted.

Hour by hour the sun and the rain, the air and the rust, and the press of time running into centuries, play on the building inside and out and use it.

Men who sunk the pilings and mixed the mortar are laid in graves where the wind whistles a wild song without words
And so are men who strung the wires and fixed the pipes and tubes and those who saw it rise floor by floor.
Souls of them all are here, even the hod carrier begging at back doors hundreds of miles away and the bricklayer who went to state's prison for shooting another man while drunk.
(One man fell from a girder and broke his neck at the end of a straight plunge—he is here—his soul has gone into the stones of the building.)

On the office doors from tier to tier—hundreds of names and each name standing for a face written across with a dead child, a passionate lover, a driving ambition for a million dollar business or a lobster's ease of life.

Behind the signs on the doors they work and the walls tell nothing from room to room.
Ten-dollar-a-week stenographers take letters from corporation officers, lawyers, efficiency engineers, and tons of letters go bundled from the building to all ends of the earth.
Smiles and tears of each office girl go into the soul of the building just the same as the master-men who rule the building.

Hands of clocks turn to noon hours and each floor empties its men and women who go away and eat and come back to work.

Toward the end of the afternoon all work slackens and all jobs go slower as the people feel day closing on them.

One by one the floors are emptied. . . The uniformed elevator men are gone. Pails clang. . . Scrubbers work, talking in foreign tongues. Broom and water and mop clean from the floors human dust and spit, and machine grime of the day.

Spelled in electric fire on the roof are words telling miles of houses and people where to buy a thing for money. The sign speaks till midnight.

Darkness on the hallways. Voices echo. Silence holds. . . Watchmen walk slow from floor to floor and try the doors. Revolvers bulge from their hip pockets. . . Steel safes stand in corners. Money is stacked in them.

A young watchman leans at a window and sees the lights of barges butting their way across a harbor, nets of red and white lanterns in a railroad yard, and a span of glooms splashed with lines of white and blurs of crosses and clusters over the sleeping city.

By night the skyscraper looms in the smoke and the stars and has a soul.

Fog

The fog comes
on little cat feet.

It sits looking
over harbor and city
on silent haunches
and then moves on.

Crimson

Crimson is the slow smolder of the cigar end I hold,
Gray is the ash that stiffens and covers all silent the fire.
(A great man I know is dead and while he lies in his coffin
    a gone flame I sit here in cumbering shadows and
    smoke and watch my thoughts come and go.)

Flux

Sand of the sea runs red
Where the sunset reaches and quivers.
Sand of the sea runs yellow
Where the moon slants and wavers.

Kin

    Brother, I am fire
Surging under the ocean floor.
I shall never meet you, brother—
Not for years, anyhow;
Maybe thousands of years, brother.
Then I will warm you,
Hold you close, wrap you in circles,
Use you and change you—
Maybe thousands of years, brother.

White Shoulders

Your white shoulders
    I remember
And your shrug of laughter.

    Low laughter
    Shaken slow
From your white shoulders.

Iron

Guns,
Long, steel guns,
Pointed from the war ships
In the name of the war god.

Straight, shining, polished guns,
Clambered over with jackies in white blouses,
Glory of tan faces, tousled hair, white teeth,
Laughing lithe jackies in white blouses,
Sitting on the guns singing war songs, war chanties.

Shovels,
Broad, iron shovels,
Scooping out oblong vaults,
Loosening turf and leveling sod.

> I ask you
> To witness—
> The shovel is brother to the gun.

Statistics

Napoleon shifted,
Restless in the old sarcophagus
And murmured to a watchguard:
"Who goes there?"
"Twenty-one million men,
Soldiers, armies, guns,
Twenty-one million
Afoot, horseback,
In the air,
Under the sea."
And Napoleon turned to his sleep:
"It is not my world answering;

It is some dreamer who knows not
'The world I marched in
From Calais to Moscow."
And he slept on
In the old sarcophagus
While the aëroplanes
Droned their motors
Between Napoleon's mausoleum
And the cool night stars.

And They Obey

Smash down the cities.
Knock the walls to pieces.
Break the factories and cathedrals, warehouses and
    homes
Into loose piles of stone and lumber and black burnt
    wood:
  You are the soldiers and we command you.

Build up the cities.
Set up the walls again.
Put together once more the factories and cathedrals,
    warehouses and homes
Into buildings for life and labor:
  You are workmen and citizens all: We command you.

Jaws

Seven nations stood with their hands on the jaws of
    death.
It was the first week in August, Nineteen Hundred Four-
    teen.
I was listening, you were listening, the whole world was
    listening,
And all of us heard a Voice murmuring:
        "I am the way and the light,
        He that believeth on me
        Shall not perish
        But shall have everlasting life."
Seven nations listening heard the Voice and answered:
        "O Hell!"
The jaws of death began clicking and they go on clicking:
        "O Hell!"

Wars

In the old wars drum of hoofs and the beat of shod feet.
In the new wars hum of motors and the tread of rubber
    tires.
In the wars to come silent wheels and whirr of rods not
    yet dreamed out in the heads of men.

In the old wars clutches of short swords and jabs into
    faces with spears.

In the new wars long range guns and smashed walls, guns
running a spit of metal and men falling in tens and
twenties.
In the wars to come new silent deaths, new silent hurlers
not yet dreamed out in the heads of men.

In the old wars kings quarreling and thousands of men
following.
In the new wars kings quarreling and millions of men
following.
In the wars to come kings kicked under the dust and mil-
lions of men following great causes not yet dreamed
out in the heads of men.

A Sphinx

Close-mouthed you sat five thousand years and never let
out a whisper.
Processions came by, marchers, asking questions you an-
swered with grey eyes never blinking, shut lips never
talking.
Not one croak of anything you know has come from your
cat crouch of ages.
I am one of those who know all you know and I keep my
questions: I know the answers you hold.

To a Dead Man

Over the dead line we have called to you
To come across with a word to us,
Some beaten whisper of what happens
Where you are over the dead line
Deaf to our calls and voiceless.

The flickering shadows have not answered
Nor your lips sent a signal
Whether love talks and roses grow
And the sun breaks at morning
Splattering the sea with crimson.

Under the Harvest Moon

Under the harvest moon,
When the soft silver
Drips shimmering
Over the garden nights,
Death, the gray mocker,
Comes and whispers to you
As a beautiful friend
Who remembers.

Under the summer roses
When the flagrant crimson
Lurks in the dusk
Of the wild red leaves,

Love, with little hands,
Comes and touches you
With a thousand memories,
And asks you
Beautiful, unanswerable questions.

Back Yard

Shine on, O moon of summer.
Shine to the leaves of grass, catalpa and oak,
All silver under your rain to-night.

An Italian boy is sending songs to you to-night from an
    accordion.
A Polish boy is out with his best girl; they marry next
    month; to-night they are throwing you kisses.

An old man next door is dreaming over a sheen that sits
    in a cherry tree in his back yard.

The clocks say I must go—I stay here sitting on the back
    porch drinking white thoughts you rain down.

      Shine on, O moon,
Shake out more and more silver changes.

On the Breakwater

On the breakwater in the summer dark, a man and a girl
    are sitting,
She across his knee and they are looking face into face
Talking to each other without words, singing rythms in
    silence to each other.

A funnel of white ranges the blue dusk from an outgoing
    boat,
Playing its searchlight, puzzled, abrupt, over a streak of
    green,
And two on the breakwater keep their silence, she on his
    knee.

I Sang

I sang to you and the moon
But only the moon remembers.
    I sang
O reckless free-hearted
                free-throated rhythms,
Even the moon remembers them
    And is kind to me.

Window

Night from a railroad car window
Is a great, dark, soft thing
Broken across with slashes of light.

Pals

Take a hold now
On the silver handles here,
Six silver handles,
One for each of his old pals.

Take hold
And lift him down the stairs,
Put him on the rollers
Over the floor of the hearse.

Take him on the last haul,
To the cold straight house,
The level even house,
To the last house of all.

   The dead say nothing
   And the dead know much
   And the dead hold under their tongues
   A locked-up story.

Child Moon

The child's wonder
At the old moon
Comes back nightly.
She points her finger
To the far silent yellow thing
Shining through the branches
Filtering on the leaves a golden sand,
Crying with her little tongue, "See the moon!"
And in her bed fading to sleep
With babblings of the moon on her little mouth.

Trafficker

Among the shadows where two streets cross,
A woman lurks in the dark and waits
To move on when a policeman heaves in view.
Smiling a broken smile from a face
Painted over haggard bones and desperate eyes,
All night she offers passers-by what they will
Of her beauty wasted, body faded, claims gone,
And no takers.

Harrison Street Court

I heard a woman's lips
Speaking to a companion
Say these words:

"A woman what hustles
Never keeps nothin'
For all her hustlin'.
Somebody always gets
What she goes on the street for.
If it ain't a pimp
It's a bull what gets it.
I been hustlin' now
Till I ain't much good any more.
I got nothin' to show for it.
Some man got it all,
Every night's hustlin' I ever did."

Jungheimer's

In western fields of corn and northern timber lands,
    They talk about me, a saloon with a soul,
    The soft red lights, the long curving bar,
    The leather seats and dim corners,
    Tall brass spittoons, a nigger cutting ham,
And the painting of a woman half-dressed thrown reck-
        less across a bed after a night of booze and riots.

Gone

Everybody loved Chick Lorimer in our town.
> Far off
> Everybody loved her.
So we all love a wild girl keeping a hold
> On a dream she wants.
Nobody knows now where Chick Lorimer went.
Nobody knows why she packed her trunk . . a few old
> things
And is gone,
> Gone with her little chin
> Thrust ahead of her
> And her soft hair blowing careless
> From under a wide hat,
Dancer, singer, a laughing passionate lover.

Were there ten men or a hundred hunting Chick?
Were there five men or fifty with aching hearts?
> Everybody loved Chick Lorimer.
> Nobody knows where she's gone.

All Day Long

All day long in fog and wind,
The waves have flung their beating crests
Against the palisades of adamant.
> My boy, he went to sea, long and long ago,
> Curls of brown were slipping underneath his cap,

He looked at me from blue and steely eyes;
Natty, straight and true, he stepped away,
My boy, he went to sea.
All day long in fog and wind,
The waves have flung their beating crests
Against the palisades of adamant.

Old Woman

The owl-car clatters along, dogged by the echo
From building and battered paving-stone;
The headlight scoffs at the mist
And fixes its yellow rays in the cold slow rain;
Against a pane I press my forehead
And drowsily look on the walls and sidewalks.

The headlight finds the way
And life is gone from the wet and the welter—
Only an old woman, bloated, disheveled and bleared.
Far-wandered waif of other days,
Huddles for sleep in a doorway,
Homeless.

'Boes

I waited today for a freight train to pass.
Cattle cars with steers butting their horns against the
    bars, went by.

And a half a dozen hoboes stood on bumpers between
cars.

Well, the cattle are respectable, I thought.

Every steer has its transportation paid for by the farmer
sending it to market,

While the hoboes are law-breakers in riding a railroad
train without a ticket.

It reminded me of ten days I spent in the Allegheny
County jail in Pittsburgh.

I got ten days even though I was a veteran of the Spanish-
American war.

Cooped in the same cell with me was an old man, a brick-
layer and a booze-fighter.

But it just happened he, too, was a veteran soldier, and he
had fought to preserve the Union and free the
niggers.

We were three in all, the other being a Lithuanian who
got drunk on pay day at the steel works and got to
fighting a policeman;

All the clothes he had was a shirt, pants and shoes—
somebody got his hat and coat and what money he
had left over when he got drunk.

I Am the People, the Mob

I am the people—the mob—the crowd—the mass.

Do you know that all the great work of the world is done
through me?

I am the workingman, the inventor, the maker of the
world's food and clothes.
I am the audience that witnesses history. The Napoleons
come from me and the Lincolns. They die. And then
I send forth more Napoleons and Lincolns.
I am the seed ground. I am a prairie that will stand for
much plowing. Terrible storms pass over me. I for-
get. The best of me is sucked out and wasted. I for-
get. Everything but Death comes to me and makes
me work and give up what I have. And I forget.
Sometimes I growl, shake myself and spatter a few red
drops for history to remember. Then—I forget.
When I, the People, learn to remember, when I, the
People, use the lessons of yesterday and no longer
forget who robbed me last year, who played me for a
fool—then there will be no speaker in all the world
say the name: "The People," with any fleck of a
sneer in his voice or any far-off smile of derision.
The mob—the crowd—the mass—will arrive then.

Languages

There are no handles upon a language
Whereby men take hold of it
And mark it with signs for its remembrance.
It is a river, this language,
Once in a thousand years
Breaking a new course
Changing its way to the ocean.

It is mountain effluvia
Moving to valleys
And from nation to nation
Crossing borders and mixing.
Languages die like rivers.
Words wrapped round your tongue today
And broken to shape of thought
Between your teeth and lips speaking
Now and today
Shall be faded hieroglyphics
Ten thousand years from now.
Sing—and singing—remember
Your song dies and changes
And is not here to-morrow
Any more than the wind
Blowing ten thousand years ago.

The Junk Man

I am glad God saw Death
And gave Death a job taking care of all who are tired of
     living:

When all the wheels in a clock are worn and slow and the
     connections loose
And the clock goes on ticking and telling the wrong time
     from hour to hour
And people around the house joke about what a bum
     clock it is,

How glad the clock is when the big Junk Man drives his
    wagon
Up to the house and puts his arms around the clock and
    says:
        "You don't belong here,
        You gotta come
        Along with me,"
How glad the clock is then, when it feels the arms of the
    Junk Man close around it and carry it away.

Silver Nails

A man was crucified. He came to the city a stranger, was accused, and nailed to a cross. He lingered hanging. Laughed at the crowd. "The nails are iron," he said. "You are cheap. In my country when we crucify we use silver nails . . ." So he went jeering. They did not understand him at first. Later they talked about him in changed voices in the saloons, bowling alleys, and churches. It came over them every man is crucified only once in his life and the law of humanity dictates silver nails be used for the job. A statue was erected to him in a public square. Not having gathered his name when he was among them, they wrote him as John Silvernail on the statue.

Prairie

I was born on the prairie and the milk of its wheat, the red of its clover, the eyes of its women, gave me a song and a slogan.

Here the water went down, the icebergs slid with gravel, the gaps and the valleys hissed, and the black loam came, and the yellow sandy loam.

Here between the sheds of the Rocky Mountains and the Appalachians, here now a morning star fixes a fire sign over the timber claims and cow pastures, the corn belt, the cotton belt, the cattle ranches.

Here the gray geese go five hundred miles and back with a wind under their wings honking the cry for a new home.

Here I know I will hanker after nothing so much as one more sunrise or a sky moon of fire doubled to a river moon of water.

The prairie sings to me in the forenoon and I know in the night I rest easy in the prairie arms, on the prairie heart.

. . .

After the sunburn of the day
handling a pitchfork at a hayrack,

after the eggs and biscuit and coffee,
the pearl-gray haystacks
in the gloaming
are cool prayers
to the harvest hands.

In the city among the walls the overland passenger train
    is choked and the pistons hiss and the wheels curse.
On the prairie the overland flits on phantom wheels and
    the sky and the soil between them muffle the pistons
    and cheer the wheels.

      · · ·

I am here when the cities are gone.
I am here before the cities come.
I nourished the lonely men on horses.
I will keep the laughing men who ride iron.
I am dust of men.

The running water babbled to the deer, the cottontail,
    the gopher.
You came in wagons, making streets and schools,
Kin of the ax and rifle, kin of the plow and horse,
Singing *Yankee Doodle*, *Old Dan Tucker*, *Turkey in the Straw*,
You in the coonskin cap at a log house door hearing a
    lone wolf howl,
You at a sod house door reading the blizzards and chi-
    nooks let loose from Medicine Hat,
I am dust of your dust, as I am brother and mother
To the copper faces, the worker in flint and clay,
The singing women and their sons a thousand years ago
Marching single file the timber and the plain.

I hold the dust of these amid changing stars.
I last while old wars are fought, while peace broods mother-like,
While new wars arise and the fresh killings of young men.
I fed the boys who went to France in great dark days.
Appomattox is a beautiful word to me and so is Valley Forge and the Marne and Verdun,
I who have seen the red births and the red deaths
Of sons and daughters, I take peace or war, I say nothing and wait.

Have you seen a red sunset drip over one of my cornfields, the shore of night stars, the wave lines of dawn up a wheat valley?
Have you heard my threshing crews yelling in the chaff of a strawpile and the running wheat of the wagonboards, my cornhuskers, my harvest hands hauling crops, singing dreams of women, worlds, horizons?

· · ·

Rivers cut a path on flat lands.
The mountains stand up.
The salt oceans press in
And push on the coast lines.
The sun, the wind, bring rain
And I know what the rainbow writes across
the east or west in a half-circle:
A love-letter pledge to come again.

· · ·

Towns on the Soo Line,
Towns on the Big Muddy,
Laugh at each other for cubs
And tease as children.

Omaha and Kansas City, Minneapolis and St. Paul, sisters
in a house together, throwing slang, growing up.
Towns in the Ozarks, Dakota wheat towns, Wichita,
Peoria, Buffalo, sisters throwing slang, growing up.

.   .   .

Out of prairie-brown grass crossed with a streamer of wig-
wam smoke—out of a smoke pillar, a blue promise—
out of wild ducks woven in greens and purples—
Here I saw a city rise and say to the peoples round world:
Listen, I am strong, I know what I want.
Out of log houses and stumps—canoes stripped from
tree-sides—flatboats coaxed with an ax from the
timber claims—in the years when the red and the
white men met—the houses and streets rose.

A thousand red men cried and went away to new places
for corn and women: a million white men came and
put up skyscrapers, threw out rails and wires, feelers
to the salt sea: now the smokestacks bite the skyline
with stub teeth.

In an early year the call of a wild duck woven in greens
and purples: now the riveter's chatter, the police
patrol, the song-whistle of the steamboat.

To a man across a thousand years I offer a handshake.
I say to him: Brother, make the story short, for the
stretch of a thousand years is short.

.   .   .

What brothers these in the dark?
What eaves of skyscrapers against a smoke moon?

These chimneys shaking on the lumber shanties
When the coal boats plow by on the river—
The hunched shoulders of the grain elevators—
The flame sprockets of the sheet steel mills
And the men in the rolling mills with their shirts off
Playing their flesh arms against the twisting wrists of
   steel:
                    what brothers these
                    in the dark
                    of a thousand years?
                         .   .   .

A headlight searches a snowstorm.
A funnel of white light shoots from over the pilot of the
      Pioneer Limited crossing Wisconsin.

In the morning hours, in the dawn,
The sun puts out the stars of the sky
And the headlight of the Limited train.

The fireman waves his hand to a country school teacher
      on a bobsled.
A boy, yellow hair, red scarf and mittens, on the bobsled,
      in his lunch box a pork chop sandwich and a V of
      gooseberry pie.

The horses fathom a snow to their knees.
Snow hats are on the rolling prairie hills.
The Mississippi bluffs wear snow hats.
                         .   .   .

Keep your hogs on changing corn and mashes of grain,
      O farmerman.

Cram their insides till they waddle on short legs
Under the drums of bellies, hams of fat.
Kill your hogs with a knife slit under the ear.
Hack them with cleavers.
Hang them with hooks in the hind legs.

. . .

A wagonload of radishes on a summer morning.
Sprinkles of dew on the crimson-purple balls.
The farmer on the seat dangles the reins on the rumps of
    dapple-gray horses.
The farmer's daughter with a basket of eggs dreams of a
    new hat to wear to the county fair.

. . .

On the left- and right-hand side of the road,
        Marching corn—
I saw it knee high weeks ago—now it is head high—
    tassels of red silk creep at the ends of the ears.

. . .

I am the prairie, mother of men, waiting.
They are mine, the threshing crews eating beefsteak, the
    farmboys driving steers to the railroad cattle pens.
They are mine, the crowds of people at a Fourth of July
    basket picnic, listening to a lawyer read the Declara-
    tion of Independence, watching the pinwheels and
    Roman candles at night, the young men and women
    two by two hunting the bypaths and kissing bridges.
They are mine, the horses looking over a fence in the
    frost of late October saying good-morning to the
    horses hauling wagons of rutabaga to market.
They are mine, the old zigzag rail fences, the new barb
    wire.

. . .

The cornhuskers wear leather on their hands.
There is no let-up to the wind.
Blue bandannas are knotted at the ruddy chins.

Falltime and winter apples take on the smolder of the
      five-o'clock November sunset: falltime, leaves, bon-
      fires, stubble, the old things go, and the earth is
      grizzled.
The land and the people hold memories, even among the
      anthills and the angleworms, among the toads and
      woodroaches—among gravestone writings rubbed
      out by the rain—they keep old things that never
      grow old.

The frost loosens corn husks.
The sun, the rain, the wind
                loosen corn husks.
The men and women are helpers.
They are all cornhuskers together.
I see them late in the western evening
            in a smoke-red dust.

                          . . .

The phantom of a yellow rooster flaunting a scarlet
      comb, on top of a dung pile crying hallelujah to the
      streaks of daylight,
The phantom of an old hunting dog nosing in the under-
      brush for muskrats, barking at a coon in a treetop at
      midnight, chewing a bone, chasing his tail round a
      corncrib,

The phantom of an old workhorse taking the steel point of a plow across a forty-acre field in spring, hitched to a harrow in summer, hitched to a wagon among cornshocks in fall,

These phantoms come into the talk and wonder of people on the front porch of a farmhouse late summer nights.

"The shapes that are gone are here," said an old man with a cob pipe in his teeth one night in Kansas with a hot wind on the alfalfa.

.   .   .

Look at six eggs
In a mockingbird's nest.

Listen to six mockingbirds
Flinging follies of O-be-joyful
Over the marshes and uplands.

Look at songs
Hidden in eggs.

.   .   .

When the morning sun is on the trumpet-vine blossoms, sing at the kitchen pans: Shout All Over God's Heaven.

When the rain slants on the potato hills and the sun plays a silver shaft on the last shower, sing to the bush at the backyard fence: Mighty Lak a Rose.

When the icy sleet pounds on the storm windows and the house lifts to a great breath, sing for the outside hills: The Ole Sheep Done Know the Road, the Young Lambs Must Find the Way.

.   .   .

Spring slips back with a girl face calling always: "Any new songs for me? Any new songs?"

O prairie girl, be lonely, singing, dreaming, waiting— your lover comes—your child comes—the years creep with toes of April rain on new-turned sod.

O prairie girl, whoever leaves you only crimson poppies to talk with, whoever puts a good-by kiss on your lips and never comes back—

There is a song deep as the falltime redhaws, long as the layer of black loam we go to, the shine of the morning star over the corn belt, the wave line of dawn up a wheat valley.

.   .   .

O prairie mother, I am one of your boys.

I have loved the prairie as a man with a heart shot full of pain over love.

Here I know I will hanker after nothing so much as one more sunrise or a sky moon of fire doubled to a river moon of water.

.   .   .

I speak of new cities and new people.

I tell you the past is a bucket of ashes.

I tell you yesterday is a wind gone down,
        a sun dropped in the west.

I tell you there is nothing in the world
        only an ocean of to-morrows,
        a sky of to-morrows.

I am a brother of the cornhuskers who say
        at sundown:
                To-morrow is a day.

Hits and Runs

I remember the Chillicothe ball players grappling the
   Rock Island ball players in a sixteen-inning game
   ended by darkness.
And the shoulders of the Chillicothe players were a red
   smoke against the sundown and the shoulders of
   the Rock Island players were a yellow smoke against
   the sundown.
And the umpire's voice was hoarse calling balls and
   strikes and outs and the umpire's throat fought in
   the dust for a song.

Village in Late Summer

Lips half-willing in a doorway.
Lips half-singing at a window.
Eyes half-dreaming in the walls.
Feet half-dancing in a kitchen.
Even the clocks half-yawn the hours
And the farmers make half-answers.

Sunset from Omaha Hotel Window

Into the blue river hills
The red sun runners go
And the long sand changes

And to-day is a goner
And to-day is not worth haggling over.

    Here in Omaha
    The gloaming is bitter
    As in Chicago
    Or Kenosha.

The long sand changes.
To-day is a goner.
Time knocks in another brass nail.
Another yellow plunger shoots the dark.

    Constellations
    Wheeling over Omaha
    As in Chicago
    Or Kenosha.

The long sand is gone
            and all the talk is stars.
They circle in a dome over Nebraska.

Still Life

Cool your heels on the rail of an observation car.
Let the engineer open her up for ninety miles an hour.
Take in the prairie right and left, rolling land and new
      hay crops, swaths of new hay laid in the sun.
A gray village flecks by and the horses hitched in front of
      the post-office never blink an eye.

A barnyard and fifteen Holstein cows, dabs of white on a
   black wall map, never blink an eye.
A signalman in a tower, the outpost of Kansas City, keeps
   his place at a window with the serenity of a bronze
   statue on a dark night when lovers pass whispering.

Band Concert

Band concert public square Nebraska city. Flowing and
   circling dresses, summer-white dresses. Faces, flesh
   tints flung like sprays of cherry blossoms. And gig-
   glers, God knows, gigglers, rivaling the pony whin-
   nies of the Livery Stable Blues.

Cowboy rags and nigger rags. And boys driving sorrel
   horses hurl a cornfield laughter at the girls in
   dresses, summer-white dresses. Amid the cornet
   staccato and the tuba oompa, gigglers, God knows,
   gigglers daffy with life's razzle dazzle.

Slow good-night melodies and Home Sweet Home. And
   the snare drummer bookkeeper in a hardware store
   nods hello to the daughter of a railroad conductor—
   a giggler, God knows, a giggler—and the summer-
   white dresses filter fanwise out of the public square.

The crushed strawberries of ice cream soda places, the
   night wind in cottonwoods and willows, the lattice
   shadows of doorsteps and porches, these know more
   of the story.

Localities

Wagon Wheel Gap is a place I never saw
And Red Horse Gulch and the chutes of Cripple Creek.

Red-shirted miners picking in the sluices,
Gamblers with red neckties in the night streets,
The fly-by-night towns of Bull Frog and Skiddoo,
The night-cool limestone white of Death Valley,
The straight drop of eight hundred feet
From a shelf road in the Hasiampa Valley:
Men and places they are I never saw.

I have seen three White Horse taverns,
One in Illinois, one in Pennsylvania,
One in a timber-hid road of Wisconsin.

I bought cheese and crackers
Between sun showers in a place called White Pigeon
Nestling with a blacksmith shop, a post-office,
And a berry-crate factory, where four roads cross.

On the Pecatonica River near Freeport
I have seen boys run barefoot in the leaves
Throwing clubs at the walnut trees
In the yellow-and-gold of autumn,
And there was a brown mash dry on the inside of their
	hands.

On the Cedar Fork Creek of Knox County
I know how the fingers of late October

Loosen the hazel nuts.
I know the brown eyes of half-open hulls.
I know boys named Lindquist, Swanson, Hildebrand.
I remember their cries when the nuts were ripe.
And some are in machine shops; some are in the navy;
And some are not on payrolls anywhere.
Their mothers are through waiting for them to come
      home.

Manitoba Childe Roland

Last night a January wind was ripping at the shingles over
      our house and whistling a wolf song under the eaves.

I sat in a leather rocker and read to a six-year-old girl the
      Browning poem, *Childe Roland to the Dark Tower
      Came*.

And her eyes had the haze of autumn hills and it was
      beautiful to her and she could not understand.

A man is crossing a big prairie, says the poem, and nothing
      happens—and he goes on and on—and it's all lone-
      some and empty and nobody home.

And he goes on and on—and nothing happens—and he
      comes on a horse's skull, dry bones of a dead horse—
      and you know more than ever it's all lonesome and
      empty and nobody home.

And the man raises a horn to his lips and blows—he fixes
a proud neck and forehead toward the empty sky and
the empty land—and blows one last wonder-cry.

And as the shuttling automatic memory of man clicks off
its results willy-nilly and inevitable as the snick of a
mouse-trap or the trajectory of a 42-centimeter
projectile,

I flash to the form of a man to his hips in snow drifts of
Manitoba and Minnesota—in the sled derby run
from Winnipeg to Minneapolis.

He is beaten in the race the first day out of Winnipeg—
the lead dog is eaten by four team mates—and the
man goes on and on—running while the other racers
ride—running while the other racers sleep—

Lost in a blizzard twenty-four hours, repeating a circle of
travel hour after hour—fighting the dogs who dig
holes in the snow and whimper for sleep—pushing
on—running and walking five hundred miles to the
end of the race—almost a winner—one toe frozen,
feet blistered and frost-bitten.

And I know why a thousand young men of the Northwest
meet him in the finishing miles and yell cheers—I
know why judges of the race call him a winner and
give him a special prize even though he is a loser.

I know he kept under his shirt and around his thudding
    heart amid the blizzards of five hundred miles that
    one last wonder-cry of Childe Roland—and I told
    the six-year-old girl all about it.

And while the January wind was ripping at the shingles
    and whistling a wolf song under the eaves, her eyes
    had the haze of autumn hills and it was beautiful to
    her and she could not understand.

Bilbea

(*From tablet writing, Babylonian excavations of 4th millennium* B C.)

Bilbea, I was in Babylon on Saturday night.
I saw nothing of you anywhere.
I was at the old place and the other girls were there, but
    no Bilbea.

Have you gone to another house? or city?
Why don't you write?
I was sorry. I walked home half-sick.

Tell me how it goes.
Send me some kind of a letter.
And take care of yourself.

Southern Pacific

Huntington sleeps in a house six feet long.
Huntington dreams of railroads he built and owned.
Huntington dreams of ten thousand men saying: Yes, sir.

Blithery sleeps in a house six feet long.
Blithery dreams of rails and ties he laid.
Blithery dreams of saying to Huntington: Yes, sir.

Huntington,
Blithery, sleep in houses six feet long.

Washerwoman

The washerwoman is a member of the Salvation Army.
And over the tub of suds rubbing underwear clean
She sings that Jesus will wash her sins away
And the red wrongs she has done God and man
Shall be white as driven snow.
Rubbing underwear she sings of the Last Great Washday.

Portrait of a Motor Car

It's a lean car . . . a long-legged dog of a car . . . a
    gray-ghost eagle car.
The feet of it eat the dirt of a road . . . the wings of it
    eat the hills.

Danny the driver dreams of it when he sees women in red
skirts and red sox in his sleep.
It is in Danny's life and runs in the blood of him . . . a
lean gray-ghost car.

Buffalo Bill

Boy heart of Johnny Jones—aching to-day?
Aching, and Buffalo Bill in town?
Buffalo Bill and ponies, cowboys, Indians?

Some of us know
All about it, Johnny Jones.

Buffalo Bill is a slanting look of the eyes,
    A slanting look under a hat on a horse.
He sits on a horse and a passing look is fixed
    On Johnny Jones, you and me, barelegged,
A slanting, passing, careless look under a hat on a horse.

Go clickety-clack, O pony hoofs along the street.
Come on and slant your eyes again, O Buffalo Bill.
Give us again the ache of our boy hearts.
Fill us again with the red love of prairies, dark nights,
    lonely wagons, and the crack-crack of rifles sput-
    tering flashes into an ambush.

Prayers of Steel

Lay me on an anvil, O God.
Beat me and hammer me into a crowbar.
Let me pry loose old walls.
Let me lift and loosen old foundations.

Lay me on an anvil, O God.
Beat me and hammer me into a steel spike.
Drive me into the girders that hold a skyscraper together.
Take red-hot rivets and fasten me into the central girders.
Let me be the great nail holding a skyscraper through
      blue nights into white stars.

Interior

In the cool of the night time
The clocks pick off the points
And the mainsprings loosen.
They will need winding.
One of these days . . .
              they will need winding.

Rabelais in red boards,
Walt Whitman in green,
Hugo in ten-cent paper covers,
Here they stand on shelves
In the cool of the night time

And there is nothing . . .
To be said against them . . .
Or for them . . .
In the cool of the night time
And the clocks.

A man in pigeon-gray pyjamas.
The open window begins at his feet
And goes taller than his head.
Eight feet high is the pattern.

Moon and mist make an oblong layout.
Silver at the man's bare feet.
He swings one foot in a moon silver.
And it costs nothing.

One more day of bread and work.
One more day . . . so much rags . . .

The man barefoot in moon silver
Mutters "You" and "You"
To things hidden
In the cool of the night time,
In Rabelais, Whitman, Hugo,
In an oblong of moon mist.

Out from the window . . . prairielands.
Moon mist whitens a golf ground.
Whiter yet is a limestone quarry.
The crickets keep on chirring.

Switch engines of the Great Western
Sidetrack box cars, make up trains
For Weehawken, Oskaloosa, Saskatchewan;
The cattle, the coal, the corn, must go
In the night . . . on the prairielands.

Chuff-chuff go the pulses.
They beat in the cool of the night time.
Chuff-chuff and chuff-chuff . . .
These heartbeats travel the night a mile
And touch the moon silver at the window
And the bones of the man.
It costs nothing.

Rabelais in red boards,
Whitman in green,
Hugo in ten-cent paper covers,
Here they stand on shelves
In the cool of the night time
And the clocks.

Psalm of Those Who Go Forth Before Daylight

The policeman buys shoes slow and careful; the teamster
buys gloves slow and careful; they take care of their
feet and hands; they live on their feet and hands.

The milkman never argues; he works alone and no one
speaks to him; the city is asleep when he is on the job;

he puts a bottle on six hundred porches and calls it a day's work; he climbs two hundred wooden stairways; two horses are company for him; he never argues.

The rolling-mill men and the sheet-steel men are brothers of cinders; they empty cinders out of their shoes after the day's work; they ask their wives to fix burnt holes in the knees of their trousers; their necks and ears are covered with a smut; they scour their necks and ears; they are brothers of cinders.

Near Keokuk

Thirty-two Greeks are dipping their feet in a creek.
Sloshing their bare feet in a cool flow of clear water.
All one midsummer day ten hours the Greeks
               stand in leather shoes shoveling gravel.
Now they hold their toes and ankles
               to the drift of running water.
Then they go to the bunk cars
               and eat mulligan and prune sauce,
Smoke one or two pipefuls, look at the stars,
               tell smutty stories
About men and women they have known,
               countries they have seen,
Railroads they have built—
               and then the deep sleep of children.

Lawyer

When the jury files in to deliver a verdict after weeks of
      direct and cross examinations, hot clashes of lawyers
      and cool decisions of the judge,
There are points of high silence—twiddling of thumbs is
      at an end—bailiffs near cuspidors take fresh chews of
      tobacco and wait—and the clock has a chance for its
      ticking to be heard.
A lawyer for the defense clears his throat and holds him-
      self ready if the word is "Guilty" to enter motion for
      a new trial, speaking in a soft voice, speaking in a
      voice slightly colored with bitter wrongs mingled
      with monumental patience, speaking with mythic
      Atlas shoulders of many preposterous, unjust cir-
      cumstances.

Three Balls

Jabowsky's place is on a side street and only the rain
      washes the dusty three balls.
When I passed the window a month ago, there rested in
      proud isolation:
A family bible with hasps of brass twisted off, a wooden
      clock with pendulum gone,
And a porcelain crucifix with the glaze nicked where the
      left elbow of Jesus is represented.
I passed to-day and they were all there, resting in proud
      isolation, the clock and the crucifix saying no more
      and no less than before, and a yellow cat sleeping in

a patch of sun alongside the family bible with the
   hasps off.
Only the rain washes the dusty three balls in front of
   Jabowsky's place on a side street.

Humdrum

If I had a million lives to live
      and a million deaths to die
      in a million humdrum worlds,
I'd like to change my name
      and have a new house number to go by
      each and every time I died
      and started life all over again.

I wouldn't want the same name every time
      and the same old house number always,
      dying a million deaths,
      dying one by one a million times:
      —would you?
                  or you?
                        or you?

Knucks

In Abraham Lincoln's city,
Where they remember his lawyer's shingle,
The place where they brought him
Wrapped in battle flags,

Wrapped in the smoke of memories
From Tallahassee to the Yukon,
The place now where the shaft of his tomb
Points white against the blue prairie dome,
In Abraham Lincoln's city . . . I saw knucks
In the window of Mister Fischman's second-hand store
On Second Street.

I went in and asked, "How much?"
"Thirty cents apiece," answered Mister Fischman.
And taking a box of new ones off a shelf
He filled anew the box in the showcase
And said incidentally, most casually
And incidentally:
"I sell a carload a month of these."

I slipped my fingers into a set of knucks,
Cast-iron knucks molded in a foundry pattern,
And there came to me a set of thoughts like these:
Mister Fischman is for Abe and the "malice to none"
        stuff,
And the street car strikers and the strike-breakers,
And the sluggers, gunmen, detectives, policemen,
Judges, utility heads, newspapers, priests, lawyers,
They are all for Abe and the "malice to none" stuff.

I started for the door.
"Maybe you want a lighter pair,"
Came Mister Fischman's voice.
I opened the door . . . and the voice again:
"You are a funny customer."

Wrapped in battle flags,
Wrapped in the smoke of memories,
This is the place they brought him,
This is Abraham Lincoln's home town.

Upstairs

I too have a garret of old playthings.
I have tin soldiers with broken arms upstairs.
I have a wagon and the wheels gone upstairs.
I have guns and a drum, a jumping-jack and a magic
    lantern.
And dust is on them and I never look at them upstairs.
I too have a garret of old playthings.

Bricklayer Love

I thought of killing myself because I am only a bricklayer
    and you a woman who loves the man who runs a
    drug store.

I don't care like I used to; I lay bricks straighter than I used
    to and I sing slower handling the trowel afternoons.

When the sun is in my eyes and the ladders are shaky and
    the mortar boards go wrong, I think of you.

Cool Tombs

When Abraham Lincoln was shoveled into the tombs, he
forgot the copperheads and the assassin . . . in the
dust, in the cool tombs.

And Ulysses Grant lost all thought of con men and Wall
Street, cash and collateral turned ashes . . . in the
dust, in the cool tombs.

Pocahontas' body, lovely as a poplar, sweet as a red haw in
November or a pawpaw in May, did she wonder?
does she remember? . . . in the dust, in the cool
tombs?

Take any streetful of people buying clothes and groceries,
cheering a hero or throwing confetti and blowing tin
horns . . . tell me if the lovers are losers . . . tell
me if any get more than the lovers . . . in the dust
. . . in the cool tombs.

Old Osawatomie

John Brown's body under the morning stars.
Six feet of dust under the morning stars.
And a panorama of war performs itself
Over the six-foot stage of circling armies.
Room for Gettysburg, Wilderness, Chickamauga,
On a six-foot stage of dust.

Grass

Pile the bodies high at Austerlitz and Waterloo.
Shovel them under and let me work—
> I am the grass; I cover all.

And pile them high at Gettysburg
And pile them high at Ypres and Verdun.
Shovel them under and let me work.
Two years, ten years, and passengers ask the conductor:
> What place is this?
> Where are we now?

> I am the grass.
> Let me work.

Gargoyle

I saw a mouth jeering. A smile of melted red iron ran over
it. Its laugh was full of nails rattling. It was a child's
dream of a mouth.

A fist hit the mouth: knuckles of gun-metal driven by an
electric wrist and shoulder. It was a child's dream of
an arm.

The fist hit the mouth over and over, again and again.
The mouth bled melted iron, and laughed its laugh-
ter of nails rattling.

And I saw the more the fist pounded the more the mouth
laughed. The fist is pounding and pounding, and the
mouth answering.

House

Two Swede families live downstairs and an Irish police-
man upstairs, and an old soldier, Uncle Joe.

Two Swede boys go upstairs and see Joe. His wife is dead,
his only son is dead, and his two daughters in Mis-
souri and Texas don't want him around.

The boys and Uncle Joe crack walnuts with a hammer on
the bottom of a flatiron while the January wind
howls and the zero air weaves laces on the window
glass.

Joe tells the Swede boys all about Chickamauga and
Chattanooga, how the Union soldiers crept in rain
somewhere a dark night and ran forward and killed
many Rebels, took flags, held a hill, and won a vic-
tory told about in the histories in school.

Joe takes a piece of carpenter's chalk, draws lines on the
floor and piles stove wood to show where six regi-
ments were slaughtered climbing a slope.

"Here they went" and "Here they went," says Joe, and
the January wind howls and the zero air weaves laces
on the window glass.

The two Swede boys go downstairs with a big blur of
guns, men, and hills in their heads. They eat herring
and potatoes and tell the family war is a wonder and
soldiers are a wonder.

One breaks out with a cry at supper: I wish we had a war
now and I could be a soldier.

Out of White Lips

Out of white lips a question: Shall seven million dead ask for their blood a little land for the living wives and children, a little land for the living brothers and sisters?

Out of white lips:—Shall they have only air that sweeps round the earth for breath of their nostrils and no footing on the dirt of the earth for their battle-drabbed, battle-soaked shoes?

Out of white lips:—Is the red in the flag the blood of a free man on a piece of land his own or is it the red of a sheep slit in the throat for mutton?

Out of white lips a white pain murmurs: Who shall have land? Him who has stood ankle deep in the blood of his comrades, in the red trenches dug in the land?

Smoke

I sit in a chair and read the newspapers.

Millions of men go to war, acres of them are buried, guns and ships broken, cities burned, villages sent up in smoke, and children where cows are killed off amid hoarse barbecues vanish like finger-rings of smoke in a north wind.

I sit in a chair and read the newspapers.

Smoke and Steel

Smoke of the fields in spring is one,
Smoke of the leaves in autumn another.
Smoke of a steel-mill roof or a battleship funnel,
They all go up in a line with a smokestack,
Or they twist . . . in the slow twist . . . of the wind.

If the north wind comes they run to the south.
If the west wind comes they run to the east.
      By this sign
      all smokes
      know each other.
Smoke of the fields in spring and leaves in autumn,
Smoke of the finished steel, chilled and blue,
By the oath of work they swear: "I know you."

Hunted and hissed from the center
Deep down long ago when God made us over,
Deep down are the cinders we came from—
You and I and our heads of smoke.
       . . . .
Some of the smokes God dropped on the job
Cross on the sky and count our years
And sing in the secrets of our numbers;
Sing their dawns and sing their evenings,

Sing an old log-fire song:

> You may put the damper up,
> You may put the damper down,
> The smoke goes up the chimney just the same.

Smoke of a city sunset skyline,
Smoke of a country dusk horizon—

> They cross on the sky and count our years.

. . . .

Smoke of a brick-red dust

> Winds on a spiral
> Out of the stacks

For a hidden and glimpsing moon.
This, said the bar-iron shed to the blooming mill,
This is the slang of coal and steel.
The day-gang hands it to the night-gang,
The night-gang hands it back.

Stammer at the slang of this—
Let us understand half of it.

> In the rolling mills and sheet mills,
> In the harr and boom of the blast fires,
> The smoke changes its shadow
> And men change their shadow;
> A nigger, a wop, a bohunk changes.

> A bar of steel—it is only

Smoke at the heart of it, smoke and the blood of a man.
A runner of fire ran in it, ran out, ran somewhere else,
And left—smoke and the blood of a man
And the finished steel, chilled and blue.

So fire runs in, runs out, runs somewhere else again,
And the bar of steel is a gun, a wheel, a nail, a shovel,
A rudder under the sea, a steering-gear in the sky;
And always dark in the heart and through it,
      Smoke and the blood of a man.
Pittsburg, Youngstown, Gary—they make their steel with
    men.

In the blood of men and the ink of chimneys
The smoke nights write their oaths:
Smoke into steel and blood into steel;
Homestead, Braddock, Birmingham, they make their
    steel with men.
Smoke and blood is the mix of steel.

     The birdmen drone
     in the blue; it is steel
     a motor sings and zooms.
      . . . .

Steel barb-wire around The Works.
Steel guns in the holsters of the guards at the gates of
    The Works.
Steel ore-boats bring the loads clawed from the earth by
    steel, lifted and lugged by arms of steel, sung on its
    way by the clanking clam-shells.
The runners now, the handlers now, are steel; they dig
    and clutch and haul; they hoist their automatic
    knuckles from job to job; they are steel making steel.
Fire and dust and air fight in the furnaces; the pour is
    timed, the billets wriggle; the clinkers are dumped:
Liners on the sea, skyscrapers on the land; diving steel in
    the sea, climbing steel in the sky.

. . . .

Finders in the dark, you Steve with a dinner bucket, you
    Steve clumping in the dusk on the sidewalks with an
    evening paper for the woman and kids, you Steve
    with your head wondering where we all end up—
Finders in the dark, Steve: I hook my arm in cinder
    sleeves; we go down the street together; it is all the
    same to us; you Steve and the rest of us end on the
    same stars; we all wear a hat in hell together, in hell
    or heaven.

    Smoke nights now, Steve.
    Smoke, smoke, lost in the sieves of yesterday;
    Dumped again to the scoops and hooks today.
    Smoke like the clocks and whistles, always.
        Smoke nights now.
        To-morrow something else.

. . . .

Luck moons come and go:
Five men swim in a pot of red steel.
Their bones are kneaded into the bread of steel:
Their bones are knocked into coils and anvils
And the sucking plungers of sea-fighting turbines.
Look for them in the woven frame of a wireless station.
So ghosts hide in steel like heavy-armed men in mirrors.
Peepers, skulkers—they shadow-dance in laughing tombs.
They are always there and they never answer.

One of them said: "I like my job, the company is good to
    me, America is a wonderful country."
One: "Jesus, my bones ache; the company is a liar; this is
    a free country, like hell."

One: "I got a girl, a peach; we save up and go on a farm
        and raise pigs and be the boss ourselves."
And the others were roughneck singers a long ways from
        home.
Look for them back of a steel vault door.

        They laugh at the cost.
        They lift the birdmen into the blue.
        It is steel a motor sings and zooms.

In the subway plugs and drums,
In the slow hydraulic drills, in gumbo or gravel,
Under dynamo shafts in the webs of armature spiders,
They shadow-dance and laugh at the cost.
            .   .   .   .

The ovens light a red dome.
Spools of fire wind and wind.
Quadrangles of crimson sputter.
The lashes of dying maroon let down.
Fire and wind wash out the slag.
Forever the slag gets washed in fire and wind.
The anthem learned by the steel is:
        Do this or go hungry.
Look for our rust on a plow.
Listen to us in a threshing-engine razz.
Look at our job in the running wagon wheat.
            .   .   .   .

Fire and wind wash at the slag.
Box-cars, clocks, steam-shovels, churns, pistons, boilers,
        scissors—

Oh, the sleeping slag from the mountains, the slag-heavy
pig-iron will go down many roads.
Men will stab and shoot with it, and make butter and
tunnel rivers, and mow hay in swaths, and slit hogs
and skin beeves, and steer airplanes across North
America, Europe, Asia, round the world.

Hacked from a hard rock country, broken and baked in
mills and smelters, the rusty dust waits
Till the clean hard weave of its atoms cripples and blunts
the drills chewing a hole in it.
The steel of its plinths and flanges is reckoned, O God, in
one-millionth of an inch.

. . . .

Once when I saw the curves of fire, the rough scarf
women dancing,
Dancing out of the flues and smoke-stacks—flying hair of
fire, flying feet upside down;
Buckets and baskets of fire exploding and chortling, fire
running wild out of the steady and fastened ovens;
Sparks cracking a harr-harr-huff from a solar-plexus of
rock-ribs of the earth taking a laugh for themselves;
Ears and noses of fire, gibbering gorilla arms of fire, gold
mud-pies, gold bird-wings, red jackets riding purple
mules, scarlet autocrats tumbling from the humps
of camels, assassinated czars straddling vermillion
balloons;
I saw then the fires flash one by one: good-by: then
smoke, smoke;
And in the screens the great sisters of night and cool
stars, sitting women arranging their hair,

Waiting in the sky, waiting with slow easy eyes, waiting
and half-murmuring:
"Since you know all
and I know nothing,
tell me what I dreamed last night."
. . . .

Pearl cobwebs in the windy rain,
in only a flicker of wind,
are caught and lost and never known again.

A pool of moonshine comes and waits,
but never waits long: the wind picks up
loose gold like this and is gone.

A bar of steel sleeps and looks slant-eyed
on the pearl cobwebs, the pools of moonshine;
sleeps slant-eyed a million years,
sleeps with a coat of rust, a vest of moths,
a shirt of gathering sod and loam.

The wind never bothers . . . a bar of steel.
The wind picks only . . pearl cobwebs . . pools
of moonshine.

Five Towns on the B. and O.

By day . . . tireless smokestacks . . . hungry smoky
shanties hanging to the slopes . . . crooning: We
get by, that's all.

By night . . . all lit up . . . fire-gold bars, fire-gold flues
. . . and the shanties shaking in clumsy shadows
. . . almost the hills shaking . . . all crooning:
By God, we're going to find out or know why.

Work Gangs

Box cars run by a mile long.
And I wonder what they say to each other
When they stop a mile long on a sidetrack.
        Maybe their chatter goes:
I came from Fargo with a load of wheat up to the danger
        line.
I came from Omaha with a load of shorthorns and they
        splintered my boards.
I came from Detroit heavy with a load of flivvers.
I carried apples from the Hood river last year and this
        year bunches of bananas from Florida; they look for
        me with watermelons from Mississippi next year.

Hammers and shovels of work gangs sleep in shop corners
when the dark stars come on the sky and the night watch-
        men walk and look.

Then the hammer heads talk to the handles,
then the scoops of the shovels talk,
how the day's work nicked and trimmed them,
how they swung and lifted all day,
how the hands of the work gangs smelled of hope.
In the night of the dark stars

when the curve of the sky is a work gang handle,
in the night on the mile long sidetracks,
in the night where the hammers and shovels sleep in
    corners,
the night watchmen stuff their pipes with dreams—
and sometimes they doze and don't care for nothin',
and sometimes they search their heads for meanings,
    stories, stars.
        The stuff of it runs like this:
A long way we come; a long way to go; long rests and
    long deep sniffs for our lungs on the way.
Sleep is a belonging of all; even if all songs are old songs
    and the singing heart is snuffed out like a switch-
    man's lantern with the oil gone, even if we forget our
    names and houses in the finish, the secret of sleep is
    left us, sleep belongs to all, sleep is the first and last
    and best of all.

People singing; people with song mouths connecting
    with song hearts; people who must sing or die;
    people whose song hearts break if there is no song
    mouth; these are my people.

Hats

        Hats, where do you belong?
          what is under you?

On the rim of a skyscraper's forehead
I looked down and saw: hats: fifty thousand hats:

Swarming with a noise of bees and sheep, cattle and
      waterfalls,
Stopping with a silence of sea grass, a silence of prairie
      corn.
                    Hats: tell me your high hopes.

They All Want to Play Hamlet

They all want to play Hamlet.
They have not exactly seen their fathers killed
Nor their mothers in a frame-up to kill,
Nor an Ophelia dying with a dust gagging the heart,
Not exactly the spinning circles of singing golden spiders,
Not exactly this have they got at nor the meaning of
      flowers—O flowers, flowers slung by a dancing girl
      —in the saddest play the inkfish, Shakespeare, ever
      wrote;
Yet they all want to play Hamlet because it is sad like all
      actors are sad and to stand by an open grave with a
      joker's skull in the hand and then to say over slow
      and say over slow wise, keen, beautiful words
      masking a heart that's breaking, breaking,
This is something that calls and calls to their blood.
They are acting when they talk about it and they know it
      is acting to be particular about it and yet: They all
      want to play Hamlet.

Manual System

Mary has a thingamajig clamped on her ears
And sits all day taking plugs out and sticking plugs in.
Flashes and flashes—voices and voices
                         calling for ears to pour words in
Faces at the ends of wires asking for other faces
                         at the ends of other wires:
All day taking plugs out and sticking plugs in,
Mary has a thingamajig clamped on her ears.

Stripes

Policeman in front of a bank 3 A.M. . . . lonely.
Policeman State and Madison . . . high noon . . .
      mobs . . . cars . . . parcels . . . lonely.

Woman in suburbs . . . keeping night watch on a
      sleeping typhoid patient . . . only a clock to talk to
      . . . lonesome.
Woman selling gloves . . . bargain day department
      store . . . furious crazy-work of many hands
      slipping in and out of gloves . . . lonesome.

Crapshooters

Somebody loses whenever somebody wins.
This was known to the Chaldeans long ago.

And more: somebody wins whenever somebody loses.
This too was in the savvy of the Chaldeans.

They take it heaven's hereafter is an eternity of crap
     games where they try their wrists years and years
     and no police come with a wagon; the game goes on
     forever.
The spots on the dice are the music signs of the songs of
     heaven here.
God is Luck: Luck is God: we are all bones the High
     Thrower rolled: some are two spots, some double
     sixes.

The myths are Phoebe, Little Joe, Big Dick.
Hope runs high with a: Huh, seven—huh, come seven
This too was in the savvy of the Chaldeans.

Cahoots

Play it across the table.
What if we steal this city blind?
If they want any thing let 'em nail it down.

Harness bulls, dicks, front office men,
And the high goats up on the bench,
Ain't they all in cahoots?
Ain't it fifty-fifty all down the line,
Petemen, dips, boosters, stick-ups and guns—
       what's to hinder?

Go fifty-fifty.
If they nail you call in a mouthpiece.
Fix it, you gazump, you slant-head, fix it.
        Feed 'em. . . .

Nothin' ever sticks to my fingers, nah, nah,
        nothin' like that,
But there ain't no law we got to wear mittens—
        huh—is there?
Mittens, that's a good one—mittens!
There oughta be a law everybody wear mittens.

The Hangman at Home

What does the hangman think about
When he goes home at night from work?
When he sits down with his wife and
Children for a cup of coffee and a
Plate of ham and eggs, do they ask
Him if it was a good day's work
And everything went well or do they
Stay off some topics and talk about
The weather, base ball, politics
And the comic strips in the papers
And the movies? Do they look at his
Hands when he reaches for the coffee
Or the ham and eggs? If the little
Ones say, Daddy, play horse, here's
A rope—does he answer like a joke:

I seen enough rope for today?
Or does his face light up like a
Bonfire of joy and does he say:
It's a good and dandy world we live
In. And if a white face moon looks
In through a window where a baby girl
Sleeps and the moon gleams mix with
Baby ears and baby hair—the hangman—
How does he act then? It must be easy
For him. Anything is easy for a hangman,
I guess.

Death Snips Proud Men

Death is stronger than all the governments because the
governments are men and men die and then death
laughs: Now you see 'em, now you don't.

Death is stronger than all proud men and so death snips
proud men on the nose, throws a pair of dice and
says: Read 'em and weep.

Death sends a radiogram every day: When I want you I'll
drop in—and then one day he comes with a master-
key and lets himself in and says: We'll go now.

Death is a nurse mother with big arms: 'Twon't hurt you
at all; it's your time now; you just need a long sleep,
child; what have you had anyhow better than sleep?

"Old-Fashioned Requited Love"

I have ransacked the encyclopedias
And slid my fingers among topics and titles
Looking for you.

And the answer comes slow.
There seems to be no answer.

I shall ask the next banana peddler the who and the why
    of it.

Or—the iceman with his iron tongs gripping a clear cube
    in summer sunlight—maybe he will know.

Osawatomie

I don't know how he came,
shambling, dark, and strong.

He stood in the city and told men:
My people are fools, my people are young and strong, my
    people must learn, my people are terrible workers
    and fighters.
Always he kept on asking: Where did that blood come
    from?

    They said: You for the fool killer,
                you for the booby hatch
                and a necktie party.

They hauled him into jail.
They sneered at him and spit on him,
And he wrecked their jails,
Singing, "God damn your jails,"
And when he was most in jail
Crummy among the crazy in the dark
Then he was most of all out of jail
Shambling, dark, and strong,
Always asking: Where did that blood come from?
They laid hands on him
And the fool killers had a laugh
And the necktie party was a go, by God.
They laid hands on him and he was a goner.
They hammered him to pieces and he stood up.
They buried him and he walked out of the grave, by God,
Asking again: Where did that blood come from?

The Lawyers Know Too Much

The lawyers, Bob, know too much.
They are chums of the books of old John Marshall.
They know it all, what a dead hand wrote,
A stiff dead hand and its knuckles crumbling,
The bones of the fingers a thin white ash.
The lawyers know
a dead man's thoughts too well.

In the heels of the higgling lawyers, Bob,
Too many slippery ifs and buts and howevers,

Too much hereinbefore provided whereas,
Too many doors to go in and out of.

> When the lawyers are through
> What is there left, Bob?
> Can a mouse nibble at it
> And find enough to fasten a tooth in?

> Why is there always a secret singing
> When a lawyer cashes in?
> Why does a hearse horse snicker
> Hauling a lawyer away?

The work of a bricklayer goes to the blue.
The knack of a mason outlasts a moon.
The hands of a plasterer hold a room together.
The land of a farmer wishes him back again.
> Singers of songs and dreamers of plays
> Build a house no wind blows over.
The lawyers—tell me why a hearse horse snickers hauling
  a lawyer's bones.

Threes

I was a boy when I heard three red words
a thousand Frenchmen died in the streets
for: Liberty, Equality, Fraternity—I asked
why men die for words.

I was older; men with mustaches, sideburns,
lilacs, told me the high golden words are:
Mother, Home, and Heaven—other older men with
face decorations said: God, Duty, Immortality
—they sang these threes slow from deep lungs.

Years ticked off their say-so on the great clocks
of doom and damnation, soup and nuts: meteors flashed
their say-so: and out of great Russia came three
dusky syllables workmen took guns and went out to die
for: Bread, Peace, Land.

And I met a marine of the U.S.A., a leatherneck with a
girl on his knee for a memory in ports circling the earth
and he said: Tell me how to say three things and I always
get by—gimme a plate of ham and eggs—how much?—
and—do you love me, kid?

A.E.F.

There will be a rusty gun on the wall, sweetheart,
The rifle grooves curling with flakes of rust.
A spider will make a silver string nest in the
                  darkest, warmest corner of it.
The trigger and the range-finder, they too will be rusty.
And no hands will polish the gun, and it will hang on the
        wall.
Forefingers and thumbs will point absently and casually
        toward it.

It will be spoken among half-forgotten, wished-to-be-
forgotten things.
They will tell the spider: Go on, you're doing good work.

Bas-Relief

Five geese deploy mysteriously.
Onward proudly with flagstaffs,
Hearses with silver bugles,
Bushels of plum-blossoms dropping
For ten mystic web-feet—
Each his own drum-major,
Each charged with the honor
Of the ancient goose nation,
Each with a nose-length surpassing
The nose-lengths of rival nations.
Somberly, slowly, unimpeachably,
Five geese deploy mysteriously.

And This Will Be All?

And this will be all?
And the gates will never open again?
And the dust and the wind will play around the rusty
door hinges and the songs of October moan, Why-
oh, why-oh?

And you will look to the mountains
And the mountains will look to you
And you will wish you were a mountain
And the mountain will wish nothing at all?
        This will be all?
The gates will never-never open again?

The dust and the wind only
And the rusty door hinges and moaning October
And Why-oh, why-oh, in the moaning dry leaves,
        This will be all?

Nothing in the air but songs
And no singers, no mouths to know the songs?
You tell us a woman with a heartache tells you it is so?
        This will be all?

Sea-Wash

The sea-wash never ends.
The sea-wash repeats, repeats.
Only old songs? Is that all the sea knows?
        Only the old strong songs?
        Is that all?
The sea-wash repeats, repeats.

Sleepyheads

Sleep is a maker of makers. Birds sleep. Feet cling to a perch. Look at the balance. Let the legs loosen, the backbone untwist, the head go heavy over, the whole works tumbles a done bird off the perch.

Fox cubs sleep. The pointed head curls round into hind legs and tail. It is a ball of red hair. It is a muff waiting. A wind might whisk it in the air across pastures and rivers, a cocoon, a pod of seeds. The snooze of the black nose is in a circle of red hair.

Old men sleep. In chimney corners, in rocking chairs, at wood stoves, steam radiators. They talk and forget and nod and are out of talk with closed eyes. Forgetting to live. Knowing the time has come useless for them to live. Old eagles and old dogs run and fly in the dreams.

Babies sleep. In flannels the papoose faces, the bambino noses, and dodo, dodo the song of many matushkas. Babies—a leaf on a tree in the spring sun. A nub of a new thing sucks the sap of a tree in the sun, yes a new thing, a what-is-it? A left hand stirs, an eyelid twitches, the milk in the belly bubbles and gets to be blood and a left hand and an eyelid. Sleep is a maker of makers.

Far Rockaway Night Till Morning

What can we say of the night?
The fog night, the moon night,
　　　　the fog moon night last night?

There swept out of the sea a song.
There swept out of the sea—
　　　　torn white plungers.
There came on the coast wind drive
In the spit of a driven spray,
On the boom of foam and rollers,
The cry of midnight to morning:
　　　　Hoi-a-loa.
　　　　Hoi-a-loa.
　　　　Hoi-a-loa.

Who has loved the night more than I have?
Who has loved the fog moon night last night
　　　　more than I have?

Out of the sea that song
　　　　—can I ever forget it?
Out of the sea those plungers
　　　　—can I remember anything else?
Out of the midnight morning cry: Hoi-a-loa:
　　　　—how can I hunt any other songs now?

Trinity Peace

The grave of Alexander Hamilton is in Trinity yard at the end of Wall Street.

The grave of Robert Fulton likewise is in Trinity yard where Wall Street stops.

And in this yard stenogs, bundle boys, scrubwomen, sit on the tombstones, and walk on the grass of graves, speaking of war and weather, of babies, wages and love.

An iron picket fence . . . and streaming thousands along Broadway sidewalks . . . straw hats, faces, legs . . . a singing, talking, hustling river . . . down the great street that ends with a Sea.

. . . easy is the sleep of Alexander Hamilton.
. . . easy is the sleep of Robert Fulton.
. . . easy are the great governments and the great steamboats.

Jack London and O. Henry

Both were jailbirds; no speechmakers at all; speaking best with one foot on a brass rail; a beer glass in the left hand and the right hand employed for gestures.

And both were lights snuffed out . . . no warning . . .
no lingering:

Who knew the hearts of these boozefighters?

Two Strangers Breakfast

The law says you and I belong to each other, George.
The law says you are mine and I am yours, George.
And there are a million miles of white snowstorms, a
      million furnaces of hell,
Between the chair where you sit and the chair where I sit.
The law says two strangers shall eat breakfast together
      after nights on the horn of an Arctic moon.

An Electric Sign Goes Dark

Poland, France, Judea ran in her veins,
Singing to Paris for bread, singing to Gotham in a fizz at
      the pop of a bottle's cork.

"Won't you come and play wiz me" she sang . . . and "I
      just can't make my eyes behave."
"Higgeldy-Piggeldy," "Papa's Wife," Follow Me" were
      plays.

Did she wash her feet in a tub of milk? Was a strand of

pearls sneaked from her trunk? The newspapers asked.

Cigarettes, tulips, pacing horses, took her name.

Twenty years old . . . thirty . . . forty . . .

Forty-five and the doctors fathom nothing, the doctors quarrel, the doctors use silver tubes feeding twenty-four quarts of blood into the veins, the respects of a prize-fighter, a cab driver.

And a little mouth moans: It is easy to die when they are dying so many grand deaths in France.

A voice, a shape, gone.

A baby bundle from Warsaw . . . legs, torso, head . . . on a hotel bed at The Savoy.

The white chiselings of flesh that flung themselves in somersaults, straddles, for packed houses:

A memory, a stage and footlights out, an electric sign on Broadway dark.

She belonged to somebody, nobody.

No one man owned her, no ten nor a thousand.

She belonged to many thousand men, lovers of the white chiseling of arms and shoulders, the ivory of a laugh, the bells of song.

Railroad brakemen taking trains across Nebraska prairies; lumbermen jaunting in pine and tamarack of the Northwest, stock ranchers in the middle west, mayors of southern cities

Say to their pals and wives now: I see by the papers Anna Held is dead.

They Buy with an Eye to Looks

The fine cloth of your love might be a fabric of Egypt,
Something Sinbad, the sailor, took away from robbers,
Something a traveler with plenty of money might pick up
And bring home and stick on the walls and say:
"There's a little thing made a hit with me
When I was in Cairo—I think I must see Cairo again
    some day."
So there are cornice manufacturers, chewing gum kings,
Young Napoleons who corner eggs or corner cheese,
Phenoms looking for more worlds to corner,
And still other phenoms who lard themselves in
And make a killing in steel, copper, permanganese,
And they say to random friends in for a call:
    "Have you had a look at my wife? Here she is.
    Haven't I got her dolled up for fair?"
O-ee! the fine cloth of your love might be a fabric of Egypt.

White Ash

There is a woman on Michigan Boulevard keeps a parrot
and goldfish and two white mice.

She used to keep a houseful of girls in kimonos and three
pushbuttons on the front door.

Now she is alone with a parrot and goldfish and two
white mice . . . but these are some of her thoughts:

The love of a soldier on furlough or a sailor on shore leave burns with a bonfire red and saffron.

The love of an emigrant workman whose wife is a thousand miles away burns with a blue smoke.

The love of a young man whose sweetheart married an older man for money burns with a sputtering uncertain flame.

And there is a love . . . one in a thousand . . . burns clean and is gone leaving a white ash. . . .

And this is a thought she never explains to the parrot and goldfish and two white mice.

Vaudeville Dancer

Elsie Flimmerwon, you got a job now with a jazz outfit in vaudeville.

The houses go wild when you finish the act shimmying a fast shimmy to The Livery Stable Blues.

It is long ago, Elsie Flimmerwon, I saw your mother over a washtub in a grape arbor when your father came with the locomotor ataxia shuffle.

It is long ago, Elsie, and now they spell your name with an electric sign.

Then you were a little thing in checked gingham and your mother wiped your nose and said: You little fool, keep off the streets.

Now you are a big girl at last and streetfuls of people read your name and a line of people shaped like a letter S stand at the box office hoping to see you shimmy.

Potomac Town in February

The bridge says: Come across, try me; see how good
    I am.
The big rock in the river says: Look at me; learn how to
    stand up.
The white water says: I go on; around, under, over, I
    go on.
A kneeling, scraggly pine says: I am here yet; they nearly
    got me last year.
A sliver of moon slides by on a high wind calling: I know
    why; I'll see you to-morrow; I'll tell you everything
    to-morrow.

Buffalo Dusk

The buffaloes are gone.
And those who saw the buffaloes are gone.
Those who saw the buffaloes by thousands and how they
    pawed the prairie sod into dust with their hoofs,
    their great heads down pawing on in a great pageant
    of dusk,
Those who saw the buffaloes are gone.
And the buffaloes are gone.

New Farm Tractor

Snub nose, the guts of twenty mules are in your cylinders
    and transmission.

The rear axles hold the kick of twenty Missouri jackasses.

It is in the records of the patent office and the ads there is
    twenty horse power pull here.

The farm boy says hello to you instead of twenty mules—
    he sings to you instead of ten span of mules.

A bucket of oil and a can of grease is your hay and oats.

Rain proof and fool proof they stable you anywhere in
    the fields with the stars for a roof.

I carve a team of long ear mules on the steering wheel—
    it's good-by now to leather reins and the songs of the
    old mule skinners.

The Skyscraper Loves Night

One by one lights of a skyscraper fling their checkering
    cross work on the velvet gown of night.
I believe the skyscraper loves night as a woman and
    brings her playthings she asks for, brings her a velvet
    gown,
And loves the white of her shoulders hidden under the
    dark feel of it all.

The masonry of steel looks to the night for somebody it
    loves,
He is a little dizzy and almost dances . . . waiting . . .
    dark . . .

Wistful

Wishes left on your lips
The mark of their wings.
Regrets fly kites in your eyes.

The Windy City

I

The lean hands of wagon men
put out pointing fingers here,
picked this crossway, put it on a map,
set up their sawbucks, fixed their shotguns,
found a hitching place for the pony express,
made a hitching place for the iron horse,
the one-eyed horse with the fire-spit head,
found a homelike spot and said, "Make a home,"
saw this corner with a mesh of rails, shuttling
    people, shunting cars, shaping the junk of
    the earth to a new city.

The hands of men took hold and tugged
And the breaths of men went into the junk
And the junk stood up into skyscrapers and asked:
Who am I? Am I a city? And if I am what is my name?
And once while the time whistles blew and blew again
The men answered: Long ago we gave you a name,
Long ago we laughed and said: You? Your name is
    Chicago.

Early the red men gave a name to a river,
    the place of the skunk,

the river of the wild onion smell,
Shee-caw-go.

Out of the payday songs of steam shovels,
Out of the wages of structural iron rivets,
The living lighted skyscrapers tell it now as a name,
Tell it across miles of sea blue water, gray blue land:
I am Chicago, I am a name given out by the breaths of
      working men, laughing men, a child, a belonging.

So between the Great Lakes,
The Grand De Tour, and the Grand Prairie,
The living lighted skyscrapers stand,
Spotting the blue dusk with checkers of yellow,
      streamers of smoke and silver,
      parallelograms of night-gray watchmen,
Singing a soft moaning song: I am a child, a belonging.

2

How should the wind songs of a windy city go?
Singing in a high wind the dirty chatter gets blown away
      on the wind—the clean shovel,
               the clean pickax,
               lasts.

It is easy for a child to get breakfast and pack off
      to school with a pair of roller skates,
      buns for lunch, and a geography.
Riding through a tunnel under a river running backward,
      to school to listen . . . how the Pottawattamies . . .
      and the Blackhawks . . . ran on moccasins . . .
      between Kaskaskia, Peoria, Kankakee, and Chicago.

It is easy to sit listening to a boy babbling
    of the Pottawattamie moccasins in Illinois,
    how now the roofs and smokestacks cover miles
    where the deerfoot left its writing
    and the foxpaw put its initials
    in the snow . . . for the early moccasins . . . to
        read.

It is easy for the respectable taxpayers to sit in the
    street cars and read the papers, faces of burglars,
    the prison escapes, the hunger strikes, the cost of
    living, the price of dying, the shop gate battles of
    strikers and strikebreakers, the strikers killing
    scabs and the police killing strikers—the strongest,
    the strongest, always the strongest.

It is easy to listen to the haberdasher customers hand
    each other their easy chatter—it is easy to die
    alive—to register a living thumbprint and be dead
    from the neck up.
And there are sidewalks polished with the footfalls of
    undertakers' stiffs, greased mannikins, wearing up-to-
    the-minute sox, lifting heels across doorsills,
    shoving their faces ahead of them—dead from the
    neck up—proud of their sox—their sox are the last
    word—dead from the neck up—it is easy.

    3

Lash yourself to the bastion of a bridge
and listen while the black cataracts of people go by,
        baggage, bundles, balloons,
        listen while they jazz the classics:

"Since when did you kiss yourself in
And who do you think you are?
Come across, kick in, loosen up.
Where do you get that chatter?"

"Beat up the short change artists.
They never did nothin' for you.
How do you get that way?
Tell me and I'll tell the world.
I'll say so, I'll say it is."

"You're trying to crab my act.
You poor fish, you mackerel,
You ain't got the sense God
Gave an oyster—it's raining—
What you want is an umbrella."

"Hush baby—
I don't know a thing.
I don't know a thing.
Hush baby."

"Hush baby,
It ain't how old you are,
It's how old you look.
It ain't what you got,
It's what you can get away with."

"Bring home the bacon.
Put it over, shoot it across.
Send 'em to the cleaners.

What we want is results, re-sults
   And damn the consequences.
        Sh . . . sh. . . .
You can fix anything
If you got the right fixers."

"Kid each other, you cheap skates.
   Tell each other you're all to the mustard—
   You're the gravy."

   "Tell 'em, honey.
Ain't it the truth, sweetheart?
   Watch your step.
   You said it.
   You said a mouthful.
We're all a lot of damn fourflushers."

  "Hush baby!
   Shoot it,
   Shoot it all!
   Coo coo, coo coo"—
This is one song of Chicago.

4

It is easy to come here a stranger and show the whole
   works, write a book, fix it all up—it is easy to come
   and go away a muddle-headed pig, a bum and a bag
   of wind.

Go to it and remember this city fished from its
   depths a text: "independent as a hog on ice."

Venice is a dream of soft waters, Vienna and Bagdad
    recollections of dark spears and wild turbans; Paris is
    a thought in Monet gray on scabbards, fabrics,
    façades; London is a fact in a fog filled with the
    moaning of transatlantic whistles; Berlin sits amid
    white scrubbed quadrangles and torn arithmetics
    and testaments; Moscow brandishes a flag and re-
    peats a dance figure of a man who walks like a bear.
Chicago fished from its depths a text: Independent
    as a hog on ice.

5

Forgive us if the monotonous houses go mile on mile
Along monotonous streets out to the prairies—
If the faces of the houses mumble hard words
At the streets—and the street voices only say:
"Dust and a bitter wind shall come."
Forgive us if the lumber porches and doorsteps
Snarl at each other—
And the brick chimneys cough in a close-up of
Each other's faces—
And the ramshackle stairways watch each other
As thieves watch—
And dooryard lilacs near a malleable iron works
Long ago languished
In a short whispering purple.

And if the alley ash cans
Tell the garbage wagon drivers
The children play the alley is Heaven
And the streets of Heaven shine

With a grand dazzle of stones of gold
And there are no policemen in Heaven—
Let the rag-tags have it their way.

And if the geraniums
In the tin cans of the window sills
Ask questions not worth answering—
And if a boy and a girl hunt the sun
With a sieve for sifting smoke—
Let it pass—let the answer be—
"Dust and a bitter wind shall come."

Forgive us if the jazz timebeats
Of these clumsy mass shadows
Moan in saxophone undertones,
And the footsteps of the jungle,
The fang cry, the rip claw hiss,
The sneak-up and the still watch,
The slant of the slit eyes waiting—
If these bother respectable people
        with the right crimp in their napkins
        reading breakfast menu cards—
        forgive us—let it pass—let be.

If cripples sit on their stumps
And joke with the newsies bawling,
"Many lives lost! many lives lost!
Ter-ri-ble ac-ci-dent! many lives lost!"—
If again twelve men let a woman go,
"He done me wrong; I shot him"—
Or the blood of a child's head

Spatters on the hub of a motor truck—
Or a 44-gat cracks and lets the skylights
Into one more bank messenger—
Or if boys steal coal in a railroad yard
And run with humped gunnysacks
While a bull picks off one of the kids
And the kid wriggles with an ear in cinders
And a mother comes to carry home
A bundle, a limp bundle,
To have his face washed, for the last time,
Forgive us if it happens—and happens again—
And happens again.

      Forgive the jazz timebeat
      of clumsy mass shadows,
      footsteps of the jungle,
      the fang cry, the rip claw hiss,
      the slant of the slit eyes waiting.

Forgive us if we work so hard
And the muscles bunch clumsy on us
And we never know why we work so hard—
If the big houses with little families
And the little houses with big families
Sneer at each other's bars of misunderstanding;
Pity us when we shackle and kill each other
And believe at first we understand
And later say we wonder why.

Take home the monotonous patter
Of the elevated railroad guard in the rush hours:

"Watch your step. Watch your step. Watch your step."
Or write on a pocket pad what a pauper said
To a patch of purple asters at a whitewashed wall:
"Let every man be his own Jesus—that's enough."

6

The wheelbarrows grin, the shovels and the mortar
    hoist an exploit.
The stone shanks of the Monadnock, the Transportation,
    the People's Gas Building, stand up and scrape
    at the sky.
The wheelbarrows sing, the bevels and the blue prints
    whisper.
The library building named after Crerar, naked
    as a stock farm silo, light as a single eagle
    feather, stripped like an airplane propeller,
    takes a path up.
Two cool new rivets say, "Maybe it is morning,"
    "God knows."

Put the city up; tear the city down;
    put it up again; let us find a city.
Let us remember the little violet-eyed
    man who gave all, praying, "Dig and
    dream, dream and hammer, till your
    city comes."

Every day the people sleep and the city dies;
    every day the people shake loose, awake and
    build the city again.

The city is a tool chest opened every day,
    a time clock punched every morning,
    a shop door, bunkers and overalls
    counting every day.

The city is a balloon and a bubble plaything
    shot to the sky every evening, whistled in
    a ragtime jig down the sunset.

The city is made, forgotten, and made again,
    trucks hauling it away haul it back
    steered by drivers whistling ragtime
    against the sunsets.

Every day the people get up and carry the city,
    carry the bunkers and balloons of the city,
    lift it and put it down.

        "I will die as many times
            as you make me over again,
            says the city to the people,
I am the woman, the home, the family,
I get breakfast and pay the rent;
I telephone the doctor, the milkman, the undertaker;
        I fix the streets
        for your first and your last ride—
Come clean with me, come clean or dirty,
I am stone and steel of your sleeping numbers;
        I remember all you forget.
        I will die as many times
        as you make me over again."

Under the foundations,
Over the roofs,
The bevels and the blue prints talk it over.
The wind of the lake shore waits and wanders.
The heave of the shore wind hunches the sand piles.
The winkers of the morning stars count out cities
And forget the numbers.

7

At the white clock-tower
lighted in night purples
over the boulevard link bridge
only the blind get by without acknowledgments.

The passers-by, factory punch-clock numbers,
      hotel girls out for the air, teameoes,
      coal passers, taxi drivers, window washers,
      paperhangers, floorwalkers, bill collectors,
      burglar alarm salesmen, massage students,
      manicure girls, chiropodists, bath rubbers,
      booze runners, hat cleaners, armhole basters,
      delicatessen clerks, shovel stiffs, work plugs—
They all pass over the bridge, they all look up
      at the white clock-tower
      lighted in night purples
      over the boulevard link bridge—
      And sometimes one says, "Well, we hand it to 'em."

Mention proud things, catalogue them.
The jack-knife bridge opening, the ore boats,
      the wheat barges passing through.

Three overland trains arriving the same hour,
    one from Memphis and the cotton belt,
    one from Omaha and the corn belt,
    one from Duluth, the lumberjack and the iron range.
Mention a carload of shorthorns taken off the valleys of
    Wyoming last week, arriving yesterday, knocked in
    the head, stripped, quartered, hung in ice boxes to-
    day, mention the daily melodrama of this humdrum,
    rhythms of heads, hides, heels, hoofs hung up.

8

It is wisdom to think the people are the city.
It is wisdom to think the city would fall to pieces
    and die and be dust in the wind.
If the people of the city all move away and leave no
    people at all to watch and keep the city.
It is wisdom to think no city stood here at all until the
    working men, the laughing men, came.
It is wisdom to think to-morrow new working men, new
    laughing men, may come and put up a new city—
Living lighted skyscrapers and a night lingo of lanterns
    testify to-morrow shall have its own say-so.

9

Night gathers itself into a ball of dark yarn.
Night loosens the ball and it spreads.
The lookouts from the shores of Lake Michigan
    find night follows day, and ping! ping! across
    sheet gray the boat lights put their signals.
Night lets the dark yarn unravel, Night speaks and
    the yarns change to fog and blue strands.

The lookouts turn to the city.
The canyons swarm with red sand lights
        of the sunset.
The atoms drop and sift, blues cross over,
        yellows plunge.
Mixed light shafts stack their bayonets;
        pledge with crossed handles.
So, when the canyons swarm, it is then the
        lookouts speak
Of the high spots over a street . . . mountain language
Of skyscrapers in dusk, the Railway Exchange,
The People's Gas, the Monadnock, the Transportation,
Gone to the gloaming.

The river turns in a half circle.
The Goose Island bridges curve
        over the river curve.
        Then the river panorama
        performs for the bridge,
        dots . . . lights . . . dots . . . lights,
        sixes and sevens of dots and lights,
        a lingo of lanterns and searchlights,
        circling sprays of gray and yellow.

10

A man came as a witness saying:
"I listened to the Great Lakes
And I listened to the Grand Prairie,
And they had little to say to each other,
A whisper or so in a thousand years.
'Some of the cities are big,' said one.

'And some not so big,' said another.
'And sometimes the cities are all gone,'
Said a black knob bluff to a light green sea."

Winds of the Windy City, come out of the prairie,
    all the way from Medicine Hat.
Come out of the inland sea blue water, come where
    they nickname a city for you.

Corn wind in the fall, come off the black lands,
    come off the whisper of the silk hangers,
    the lap of the flat spear leaves.

Blue water wind in summer, come off the blue miles
    of lake, carry your inland sea blue fingers,
    carry us cool, carry your blue to our homes.

White spring winds, come off the bag wool clouds,
    come off the running melted snow, come white
    as the arms of snow-born children.

Gray fighting winter winds, come along on the tear-
    ing blizzard tails, the snouts of the hungry
    hunting storms, come fighting gray in winter.

Winds of the Windy City,
Winds of corn and sea blue,
Spring wind white and fighting winter gray,
Come home here—they nickname a city for you.

The wind of the lake shore waits and wanders.
The heave of the shore wind hunches the sand piles.
The winkers of the morning stars count out cities
And forget the numbers.

At the Gates of Tombs

Civilizations are set up and knocked down
the same as pins in a bowling alley.

Civilizations get into the garbage wagons
and are hauled away the same as potato
peelings or any pot scrapings.

Civilizations, all the work of the artists,
inventors, dreamers of work and genius,
go to the dumps one by one.

Be silent about it; since at the gates of tombs
silence is a gift, be silent; since at the epitaphs
written in the air, since at the swan songs hung in
the air, silence is a gift, be silent; forget it.

If any fool, babbler, gabby mouth, stand up and say:
Let us make a civilization where the sacred and
beautiful things of toil and genius shall last—

If any such noisy gazook stands up and makes himself
heard—put him out—tie a can on him—lock him up
in Leavenworth—shackle him in the Atlanta hoosegow

—let him eat from the tin dishes at Sing Sing—
slew him in as a lifer at San Quentin.

It is the law; as a civilization dies and goes down
to eat ashes along with all other dead civilizations
—it is the law all dirty wild dreamers die first—
gag 'em, lock 'em up, get 'em bumped off.

And since at the gates of tombs silence is a gift,
be silent about it, yes, be silent—forget it.

Hazardous Occupations

Jugglers keep six bottles in the air.
Club swingers toss up six and eight.
The knife throwers miss each other's
        ears by a hair and the steel quivers
        in the target wood.
The trapeze battlers do a back-and-forth
        high in the air with a girl's feet
        and ankles upside down.
So they earn a living—till they miss
        once, twice, even three times.
So they live on hate and love as gypsies
        live in satin skins and shiny eyes.
In their graves do the elbows jostle once
        in a blue moon—and wriggle to throw
        a kiss answering a dreamed-of applause?
Do the bones repeat: It's a *good* act—
        we got a *good* hand . . . ?

Props

1

Roll open this rug; a minx is
in it; see her toe wiggling;
roll open the rug; she is a
runaway; or somebody is trying
to steal her; here she is;
here's your minx; how can we
have a play unless we have
this minx?

2

The child goes out in the storm
stage thunder; "erring daughter,
never darken this door-sill again";
the tender parents speak their curse;
the child puts a few knick-knacks in
a handkerchief; and the child goes;
the door closes and the child goes;
she is out now, in the storm on the
stage, out forever; snow, you son-of-a-gun,
snow, turn on the snow.

Ambassadors of Grief

There was a little fliv of a woman loved one man and lost out. And she took up with another and it was a blank again. And she cried to God the whole layout was a fake and a frame-up. And when she took up with Number Three she found the fires burnt out, the love power, gone. And she wrote a letter to God and dropped it in a mail-box. The letter said:

O God, ain't there some way you can fix it up so the little flivs of women, ready to throw themselves in front of railroad trains for men they love, can have a chance? I guessed the wrong keys, I battered on the wrong panels, I picked the wrong roads. O God, ain't there no way to guess again and start all over back where I had the keys in my hands, back where the roads all came together and I had my pick?

And the letter went to Washington, D.C., dumped into a dump where all letters go addressed to God—and no house number.

FROM **Good Morning, America**

15

In God we trust; it is so written.

The writing goes onto every silver dollar.

The fact: God is the great One who made us all.

We is you and me and all of us in the United States of America.

And trusting God means we give ourselves, all of ourselves, the whole United States of America, to God, the great One.

Yes . . . perhaps . . . is that so?

16

The silent litany of the workmen goes on—

Speed, speed, we are the makers of speed.

We make the flying, crying motors,

Clutches, brakes, and axles,

Gears, ignitions, accelerators,

Spokes and springs and shock absorbers.

The silent litany of the workmen goes on—

Speed, speed, we are the makers of speed;

Axles, clutches, levers, shovels,

We make the signals and lay the way—

Speed, speed.

The trees come down to our tools.
We carve the wood to the wanted shape.
The whining propeller's song in the sky,
The steady drone of the overland truck,
Comes from our hands; us; the makers of speed.

Speed; the turbines crossing the Big Pond,
Every nut and bolt, every bar and screw,
Every fitted and whirling shaft,
They came from us, the makers,
Us, who know how,
Us, the high designers and the automatic feeders,
Us, with heads,
Us, with hands,
Us, on the long haul, the short flight,
We are the makers; lay the blame on us—
The makers of speed.

Small Homes

The green bug sleeps in the white lily ear.
The red bug sleeps in the white magnolia.
Shiny wings, you are choosers of color.
You have taken your summer bungalows wisely.

Milk-White Moon, Put the Cows to Sleep

Milk-white moon, put the cows to sleep.
Since five o'clock in the morning,
Since they stood up out of the grass,
Where they slept on their knees and hocks,
They have eaten grass and given their milk
And eaten grass again and given milk,
And kept their heads and teeth at the earth's face.
    Now they are looking at you, milk-white moon.
    Carelessly as they look at the level landscapes,
    Carelessly as they look at a pail of new white milk,
    They are looking at you, wondering not at all, at all,
    If the moon is the skim face top of a pail of milk,
    Wondering not at all, carelessly looking.
    Put the cows to sleep, milk-white moon,
    Put the cows to sleep.

Slow Program

The iron rails run into the sun.
The setting of the sun chooses an hour.
The red rail ribbons run into the red ball sun.
The ribbons and the ball change like red water lights.
The picture floats with a slow program of red haze
    lights.

Three Slants at New York

New York is a city of many cats.
Some say New York is Babylon.
There is a rose and gold mist New York.

New York is a city of many cats; they eat the swill of the poor and the swell swill; they rub their backs against fire escapes and weep to each other from alley barrels; they are born to the cat life of New York.

Some say New York is Babylon; here are Babylonian dancers stripped to the flash of the navel, while the waiters murmur, "Yes," in undertones to regular customers calling for the same whiskey as last time; and having seen a thing of much preparation, toil and genius, having spoken to each other of how marvelous it is, they eat and drink till it is forgotten; and the topics are easy topics, such as which bootleggers take the biggest risks, and what light risks superior bootleggers travel under.

There is a rose and gold New York of evening lights and sunsets; there is a mist New York seen from steamboats, a massed and spotted hovering ghost, a shape the fists of men have lifted out of dirt and work and daylight and early morning oaths after sleep nights.

New York is a city of many cats.
Some say New York is Babylon.
There is a rose and gold mist New York.

Phizzog

This face you got,
This here phizzog you carry around,
You never picked it out for yourself,
    at all, at all—did you?
This here phizzog—somebody handed it
    to you—am I right?
Somebody said, "Here's yours, now go see
    what you can do with it."
Somebody slipped it to you and it was like
    a package marked:
"No goods exchanged after being taken away"—
This face you got.

Two Nocturns

1

The sea speaks a language polite people never repeat.
It is a colossal scavenger slang and has no respect.
Is it a terrible thing to be lonely?

2

The prairie tells nothing unless the rain is willing.
It is a woman with thoughts of her own.
Is it a terrible thing to love much?

They Met Young

1

"I could cry for roses, thinking of you,
Thinking of your lips, so like roses,
Thinking of the meetings of lips
And the crying of eyes meeting."

"I could love you in shadows, drinking
Of you, drinking till a morning sun.
I could touch the young heart of you
And learn all your red songs."

"I could answer the metronomes of blood,
The timebeats of your sweet kisses.
I could sing a star song or a sun song
In the crying of eyes meeting."

2

"Give me your lips.
Let Egypt come or Egypt go.
Open a window of stars.
Let a bag of shooting stars fall.
Wind us with a winding silk.
Pick us a slouching, foolish moon.
Take us to a silver blue morning.
It is too much—let your lips go.
The hammers call, the laws of the
        hammers knock on gongs, beat and
        beat on gongs.
It is too much—give me your lips
        —let your lips go."

17

"The people is a myth, an abstraction."
And what myth would you put in place
of the people?
And what abstraction would you exchange
for this one?
And when has creative man not toiled
deep in myth?
And who fights for a bellyful only and
where is any name worth remembering
for anything else than the human ab-
straction woven through it with in-
visible thongs?
"Precisely who and what is the people?"
Is this far off from asking what is grass?
what is salt? what is the sea? what is
loam?
What are seeds? what is a crop? why must
mammals have milk soon as born or they
perish?
And how did that alfalfaland governor
mean it: "The common people is a mule
that will do anything you say except
stay hitched"?

19

The people, yes, the people,
Everyone who got a letter today
And those the mail-carrier missed,
The women at the cookstoves preparing meals,
in a sewing corner mending, in a basement
laundering, woman the homemaker,
The women at the factory tending a stitching
machine, some of them the mainstay of the
jobless man at home cooking, laundering,
Streetwalking jobhunters, walkers alive and keen,
sleepwalkers drifting along, the stupefied and
hopeless down-and-outs, the game fighters
who will die fighting,
Walkers reading signs and stopping to study
windows, the signs and windows aimed
straight at their eyes, their wants,
Women in and out of doors to look and feel, to
try on, to buy and take away, to order and
have it charged and delivered, to pass by on
account of price and conditions,
The shopping crowds, the newspaper circulation,
the bystanders who witness parades, who
meet the boat, the train, who throng in
wavelines to a fire, an explosion, an accident—
The people, yes—
Their shoe soles wearing holes in stone steps, their
hands and gloves wearing soft niches in ban-
isters of granite, two worn foot-tracks at the
general-delivery window,

Driving their cars, stop and go, red light, green
        light, and the law of the traffic cop's fingers,
        on their way, loans and mortgages, margins to
        cover,
Payments on the car, the bungalow, the radio, the
        electric icebox, accumulated interest on loans
        for past payments, the writhing point of
        where the money will come from,
Crime thrown in their eyes from every angle,
        crimes against property and person, crime in
        the prints and films, crime as a lurking
        shadow ready to spring into reality, crime as
        a method and a technic,
Comedy as an offset to crime, the laughmakers,
        the odd numbers in the news and the movies,
        original clowns and imitators, and in the best
        you never know what's coming next even
        when it's hokum,
And sports, how a muff in the seventh lost yes-
        terday's game and now they are learning to
        hit Dazzy's fadeaway ball and did you hear
        how Foozly plowed through that line for a
        touchdown this afternoon?
And daily the death toll of the speed wagons; a
        cripple a minute in fenders, wheels, steel and
        glass splinters; a stammering witness before a
        coroner's jury, "It happened so sudden I
        don't know what happened."
And in the air a decree: life is a gamble; take a
        chance; you pick a number and see what you

get: anything can happen in this sweepstakes:
around the corner may be prosperity or the
worst depression yet: who knows? nobody:
you pick a number, you draw a card, you
shoot the bones.

In the poolrooms the young hear, "Ashes to
ashes, dust to dust, If the women don't get
you then the whiskey must," and in the
churches, "We walk by faith and not by sight,"

Often among themselves in their sessions of can-
dor the young saying, "Everything's a racket,
only the gyp artists get by."

And over and beyond the latest crime or comedy
always that relentless meal ticket saying
dont-lose-me, hold your job, glue your mind
on that job or when your last nickel is gone
you live on your folks or sign for relief,

And the terror of these unknowns is a circle of
black ghosts holding men and women in toil
and danger, and sometimes shame, beyond
the dreams of their blossom days, the days
before they set out on their own.

What is this "occupational disease" we hear
about? It's a sickness that breaks your health
on account of the work you're in. That's all.
Another kind of work and you'd have been
as good as any of them. You'd have been
your old self.

And what is this "hazardous occupation"? Why
that's where you're liable to break your neck

or get smashed on the job so you're no good
on that job any more and that's why you
can't get any regular life insurance so long as
you're on that job.
These are heroes then—among the plain people—
Heroes, did you say? And why not? They
give all they've got and ask no questions and
take what comes and what more do you
want?
On the street you can see them any time, some
with jobs, some nothing doing, here a down-
and-out, there a game fighter who will die
fighting.

21

Who knows the people, the migratory harvest hands and
berry pickers, the loan shark victims, the installment
house wolves,
The jugglers in sand and wood who smooth their hands
along the mold that casts the frame of your motor-
car engine,
The metal polishers, solderers, and paint spray hands
who put the final finish on the car,
The riveters and bolt-catchers, the cowboys of the air in
the big city, the cowhands of the Great Plains, the
ex-convicts, the bellhops, redcaps, lavatory men—
The union organizer with his list of those ready to join
and those hesitating, the secret paid informers who
report every move toward organizing,

The house-to-house canvassers, the doorbell ringers, the good-morning-have-you-heard boys, the strike pickets, the strikebreakers, the hired sluggers, the ambulance crew, the ambulance chasers, the picture chasers, the meter readers, the oysterboat crews, the harborlight tenders—

who knows the people?

Who knows this from pit to peak? The people, yes.

Brim

Brim's hammer hit a wheelbarrow; a sliver of iron sent itself through the lens of the eye into the eyeball.

Brim in the white sheets wonders if he will lose an eye and if a wedding is put off when a woman says a one-eyed man won't do.

The doc says maybe the eye will last; the doc X-rays, goes in with a knife, holds the slit with wires, pulls the sliver out with a magnet, stitches the eyeball, and says a week later the eye is saved.

Brim knows now the wedding comes off; among the white sheets with one eye dark he knows his sweetheart will not face a one-eyed man at the breakfasts of life's years.

A month; the doc knows the eye is lost; the doc is thinking; it is not so easy to tell a man one eye is lost; still more it is not so easy to tell a man what must be told again to a woman who wonders whether it will pay her to have a one-eyed man to eat breakfast with all along life's years.

Brim is in the white sheets thinking; the doc is in his
office thinking; the woman . . . the woman. . . .

1928

François Villon Forgotten

The women of the city where I was forgotten,
The dark-eyed women who forgot me heard me singing
And it helped them the more to be forgetting
And I sang and sang on helping them to forget
In the city where I sang to be forgotten.

I slept with a woman ten men had forgotten.
She said I'd forget her and she'd forget me.
She said the two of us could sing one song
        On how bitter yesterday was
And another on tomorrow more bitter yet.
The two of us sang these songs.

Five women said they would forget me,
Since I sang with a heart half-broken,
Since I sang like a man expecting nothing.
        Five women have forgotten me.
        Ask them and they answer:
        He's dim as mist to remember
            and oh he's long gone.

1920

The Hammer

I have seen
The old gods go
And the new gods come.

Day by day
And year by year
The idols fall
And the idols rise.

Today
I worship the hammer.

1910

Hammers Pounding

Grant had a sledgehammer pounding and pounding and
Lee had a sledgehammer pounding and pounding
And the two hammers gnashed their ends against each
other and broke holes and splintered and withered
And nobody knew how the war would end and everybody
prayed God his hammer would last longer than the
other hammer
Because the whole war hung on the big guess of who had
the hardest hammer
And in the end one side won the war because it had a
harder hammer than the other side.

Give us a hard enough hammer, a long enough hammer,
   and we will break any nation,
Crush any star you name or smash the sun and the moon
   into small flinders.

1915

Dust

Here is dust remembers it was a rose
   one time and lay in a woman's hair.
Here is dust remembers it was a woman
   one time and in her hair lay a rose.
Oh things one time dust, what else now is it
   you dream and remember of old days?

1913

We Must Be Polite

(Lessons for children on how to behave under peculiar circumstances)

1

If we meet a gorilla
what shall we do?

Two things we may do
if we so wish to do.

Speak to the gorilla,
very, very respectfully,
"How do you do, sir?"

Or, speak to him with less
distinction of manner,
"Hey, why don't you go back
where you came from?"

2

If an elephant knocks on your door
and asks for something to eat,
there are two things to say:

Tell him there are nothing but cold
victuals in the house and he will do
better next door.

Or say: We have nothing but six bushels
of potatoes—will that be enough for
your breakfast, sir?

Two Moon Fantasies

1

She bade the moon stand still.
And the moon stood still for her,
At her request came to a stillstand.
"I am in love," she was saying.
She reached up with a single finger,

Pushed the moon with one little finger
And put the moon where she wanted it.
"I am in love," she was saying.
>On a later day, far later,
>She found her magic lacking.
>The moon was the same
>And her one finger the same
>Yet nothing happened.
And her laughter rang glad as she cried:
>"It was a good trick while it lasted."

2

The moon is a bucket of suds
yellow and smooth suds.
The horses of the moon dip their heads
into this bucket and drink.
The cats of the moon, the dogs, the rats,
they too go to this bucket for drink.
Thus an apparition told it.
To him the moon meant drink and drinkers.

The moon is a disc of hidden books.
Reach an arm into it
and feel around with your hands
and you bring out books already written
and many books yet to be written
for the moon holds past, present, future.
Thus an apparition related the matter.
To him the disc meant print and printers.

Billy Sunday

You come along—tearing your shirt—yelling about Jesus.
    I want to know what the hell you know about Jesus?

Jesus had a way of talking soft, and everybody except a
    few bankers and higher-ups among the con men of
    Jerusalem liked to have this Jesus around because
    he never made any fake passes, and everything he
    said went and he helped the sick and gave the
    people hope.

You come along squirting words at us, shaking your fist
    and calling us all dam fools—so fierce the froth of
    your own spit slobbers over your lips—always
    blabbering we're all going to hell straight off and
    you know all about it.

I've read Jesus' words. I know what he said. You don't
    throw any scare into me. I've got your number. I
    know how much you know about Jesus.

He never came near clean people or dirty people but
    they felt cleaner because he came along. It was your
    crowd of bankers and business men and lawyers that
    hired the sluggers and murderers who put Jesus out
    of the running.

I say it was the same bunch that's backing you that nailed
   the nails into the hands of this Jesus of Nazareth.
   He had lined up against him the same crooks and
   strong-arm men now lined up with you paying
   your way.

This Jesus guy was good to look at, smelled good,
   listened good. He threw out something fresh and
   beautiful from the skin of his body and the touch
   of his hands wherever he passed along.

You, Billy Sunday, put a smut on every human blossom
   that comes in reach of your rotten breath belching
   about hell-fire and hiccuping about this man who
   lived a clean life in Galilee.

When are you going to quit making the carpenters build
   emergency hospitals for women and girls driven
   crazy with wrecked nerves from your goddam
   gibberish about Jesus? I put it to you again:
   What the hell do you know about Jesus?

Go ahead and bust all the chairs you want to. Smash a
   wagon load of furniture at every performance.
   Turn sixty somersaults and stand on your nutty
   head. If it wasn't for the way you scare the women
   and kids, I'd feel sorry for you and pass the hat.

I like to watch a good four-flusher work, but not when
   he starts people puking and calling for the doctor.

I like a man that's got guts and can pull off a great, original performance; but you—hell, you're only a bughouse peddler of second-hand gospel—you're only shoving out a phoney imitation of the goods this Jesus guy told us ought to be free as air and sunlight.

Sometimes I wonder what sort of pups born from mongrel bitches there are in the world less heroic, less typic of historic greatness than you.

You tell people living in shanties Jesus is going to fix it up all right with them by giving them mansions in the skies after they're dead and the worms have eaten 'em.

You tell $6 a week department store girls all they need is Jesus; you take a steel trust wop, dead without having lived, gray and shrunken at forty years of age, and you tell him to look at Jesus on the cross and he'll be all right.

You tell poor people they don't need any more money on pay day, and even if it's fierce to be out of a job, Jesus'll fix that all right, all right—all they gotta do is take Jesus the way you say.

I'm telling you this Jesus guy wouldn't stand for the stuff you're handing out. Jesus played it different. The bankers and corporation lawyers of Jerusalem got their sluggers and murderers to go after Jesus just

because Jesus wouldn't play their game. He didn't
    sit in with the big thieves.

I don't want a lot of gab from a bunkshooter in my
    religion.

I won't take my religion from a man who never works
    except with his mouth and never cherishes a
    memory except the face of the woman on the
    American silver dollar.

I ask you to come through and show me where you're
    pouring out the blood of your life.

I've been out to this suburb of Jerusalem they call
    Golgotha, where they nailed Him, and I know if
    the story is straight it was real blood ran from his
    hands and the nail-holes, and it was real blood
    spurted out where the spear of the Roman soldier
    rammed in between the ribs of this Jesus of
    Nazareth.

God's Children

   I hear Billy Sunday
   And the Kaiser and the Czar
   Talking about God
Like God was some pal of theirs,
Like the rest of us was in the cold outside,

Like they had been drinking beer with God,
Like as though they know whether God
Calls for a short beer or a gin fizz
Or whether God sleeps in a Y.M.C.A. dormitory
And never goes near a booze bazaar.

When I listen to Billy Sunday
Holler out loud
How God "hates a quitter,"
How God "hates a mutt,"
I can't help it—I feel just like God was some cheap dirty
     thing born from a fiddler's bitch and kicked from
     one back door to another.

Jerry

Six years I worked in a knitting mill at a machine
And then I married Jerry, the iceman, for a change.
He weighed 240 pounds, and could hold me,
Who weighed 105 pounds, outward easily with one
     hand.
He came home drunk and lay on me with the breath of
     stale beer
Blowing from him and jumbled talk that didn't mean
     anything.
I stood it two years and one hot night when I refused
     him
And he struck his bare fist against my nose so it bled,

I waited till he slept, took a revolver from a bureau
    drawer,
Placed the end of it to his head and pulled the trigger.
From the stone walls where I am incarcerated for the
    natural term
Of life, I proclaim I would do it again.

Black Prophetess

I makes my livin' washin'.
I keeps happy at the feet of Jesus.
My husband ain't saved; he's wicked:
but the Bible says a sanctified wife
shall sanctify her husband and save him.

I'm livin' in Chicago
but I calls Ohio my home
because I lived in Cincinnati
an' Columbus an' Toledo
an' I was in Dayton
a week before the waters swept Dayton
an' I stood on the public square
an' warned 'em of destruction.

I got four permits from the police in Chicago
to stand on the street corners
and warn the people of destruction.
I told 'em about the *Eastland* and the war
before those things happened.

Three years ago the police gave me my last permit
to warn the people of destruction
an' I got a right to stand on any corner
south of Twelfth Street.

They tell me it's a free country
an' I can talk God's destruction all I want
just so I don't come downtown.

I got five daughters.
The oldest is in Philadelphia.
She makes prophecies too.

I make prophecies when the spirit moves me.
Yesterday I felt the spirit stirrin' me up.
I saw blood up to the bridles of the horses.
I saw the mark of the Beast.
(When the Bible speaks of a Beast it means a King.)
The Kings all got to go.

God is cleansing the earth.
He's goin' to make it all clean
and Jesus is goin' to come again
an' live a thousand years.

I go to the newspapers with my prophecies
but they don't print 'em.

If you print this—
when will it be in the paper?

BIOGRAPHICAL NOTE

Carl August Sandburg was born on January 6, 1878, in Gales-
burg, Illinois, the son of Swedish immigrants. He left school at
thirteen and worked as farmhand, dishwasher, and at other odd
jobs. After serving in the Spanish-American War in Puerto Rico
in 1898, he enrolled at Lombard College in Illinois, where he
began to write poetry. He worked for Wisconsin's Social Demo-
cratic Party (1907–12) and as secretary to Milwaukee's Socialist
mayor Emil Seidel. He married Lilian Steichen (sister of pho-
tographer Edward Steichen) in 1908. Moving to Chicago in
1912, he wrote for the *Chicago Evening World* and the Chicago
Daily News. His many collections of poetry included *Chicago
Poems* (1916), *Cornhuskers* (1918), *Smoke and Steel* (1920), *Slabs
of the Sunburnt West* (1922), *Good Morning, America* (1928), and
The People, Yes (1936). His multi-volume biography of Abraham
Lincoln was published in 1926 and 1939. He won the Pulitzer
Prize for *Collected Poems* in 1951. He lectured frequently, gave
public performances of folk songs, and collaborated with
Edward Steichen on the photographic exhibit *The Family of Man*.
His final volume of poetry, *Honey and Salt*, was published in
1963. He died on July 22, 1967.

NOTE ON THE TEXTS

The texts of the poems printed in this volume are taken from their first publication in one of Carl Sandburg's books, listed as follows:

Chicago Poems (New York: Holt, 1916).

Cornhuskers (New York: Holt, 1918).

Smoke and Steel (New York: Harcourt, Brace & Howe, 1920).

Slabs of the Sunburnt West (New York: Harcourt, Brace, 1922).

Good Morning, America (New York: Harcourt, Brace, 1928).

The People, Yes (New York: Harcourt, Brace, 1936).

Complete Poems (New York: Harcourt, Brace, 1950).

The texts for the poems in the "Uncollected Poems" section, not published during Sandburg's lifetime, are taken from George Hendrick and Willene Hendrick (eds.), *Billy Sunday and Other Poems* (New York: Harvest, 1993).

The texts of the original printings chosen for inclusion here are presented without change, except for the correction of typographical errors. Spelling, punctuation, and capitalization are often expressive features and are not altered, even when inconsistent or irregular. The following errors have been corrected: 10.14–15, anothers'; 16.5 & 22, trapsing; 30.18, rythms; 39.13, said,"; 84.11, Ossawatomie; 109.18, "I; 109.23, "Come; 120.1, Milk White.

INDEX OF TITLES
AND FIRST LINES

AMERICAN POETS PROJECT